I0689930

George Brinley, Nathaniel Paine

List of books received by the American antiquarian society

from the sale of the first part of the Brinley library

George Brinley, Nathaniel Paine

List of books received by the American antiquarian society from the sale of the first part of the Brinley library

ISBN/EAN: 9783337713423

Printed in Europe, USA, Canada, Australia, Japan

Cover: Foto ©ninafisch / pixelio.de

More available books at **www.hansebooks.com**

LIST OF BOOKS

RECEIVED BY THE

AMERICAN ANTIQUARIAN SOCIETY

FROM THE SALE OF THE FIRST PART OF THE

BRINLEY LIBRARY;

TO WHICH IS ADDED A CATALOGUE OF THE MATHER PUBLICATIONS
PREVIOUSLY IN THE SOCIETY'S LIBRARY.

Worcester:
PRESS OF CHARLES HAMILTON.
1879.

Z 202
.P15

BOOKS

RECEIVED BY THE

AMERICAN ANTIQUARIAN SOCIETY

FROM THE LIBRARY OF THE LATE GEORGE BRINLEY.

UNDOUBTEDLY the most valuable gift of books to the Antiquarian Society, since that of its founder, Isaiah Thomas, is that lately received from the heirs of the late George Brinley of Hartford, Conn. The circumstances attending this generous gift will be best understood by reading the following letter from the administrators of Mr. Brinley's estate :—

HARTFORD, CONN., *Feb.* 24, 1879.

TO THE HON. STEPHEN SALISBURY, LL.D.,
President of the American Antiquarian Society.

DEAR SIR:—The late Mr. George Brinley of Hartford, when he decided that his American Library should be sold by auction, intended to give certain institutions and societies, which he designated, the opportunity of obtaining at the sale, free of cost, such of his books as they should respectively select for their libraries to the value in the aggregate of twenty-five thousand dollars.

Though this intention was not expressed in Mr. Brinley's last will, and his widow's purpose to ratify the gifts by a formal bequest was defeated by her decease intestate, his and her children take pleasure in giving the intention effect, and you are hereby informed that the American Antiquarian Society is authorized to bid off, at the sales of the Brinley Library, books for the library of the Society to the amount of five thousand dollars ($5,000), and that one-half of this amount—or a less proportion, at your option—may be so taken from the *First Part* of the Library, which is to be sold in New York, on the tenth day of March next and days following, by Messrs. Geo. A. Leavitt & Co., auctioneers. A copy of the sale-catalogue is herewith forwarded to you.

As soon as practicable after the sale you will please furnish us with a statement of the amount to which books shall have been so bid off for you, and thereupon a proper credit for this amount will be arranged for you with the auctioneers.

We are, very respectfully,

Your obed't serv'ts,

G. P. BRINLEY,

J. HAMMOND TRUMBULL,

Administrators.

To this very liberal offer, voluntarily made by the children of Mr. Brinley, to carry into effect plans formed by him, but which had not been legally completed, the following response was made in behalf of the Antiquarian Society by the President:—

[A COPY.]

AMERICAN ANTIQUARIAN SOCIETY,

WORCESTER, *Feb.* 27, 1879.

GEORGE P. BRINLEY, Esq.,

J. HAMMOND TRUMBULL, LL.D.,

Administrators of the Estate of late George Brinley, Esq.

GENTLEMEN:—In behalf of the American Antiquarian Society I thankfully acknowledge your favor of 24th inst. communicating the offer of the heirs of George Brinley, Esq., to that Society of the privilege of bidding off, free of cost, at the auction of the library of Mr. Brinley, on March 10, books for the library of that Society to the amount of $5,000. The Society will avail themselves of this privilege with a deep sense of their obligation to a friend to whom they have before been repeatedly indebted. The Society fully and gratefully appreciate the wisdom of Mr. Brinley in an arrangement most favorable to the largest usefulness of his excellent collection, and the good judgment and generosity of his family in carrying out his plan.

Very respectfully yours,

STEPHEN SALISBURY.

The balance of the gift referred to in the letter of the administrators, was divided as follows: To the library of Yale College, $10,000; the Watkinson Library of Hartford, Conn., $5,000, and the New York Historical Society and Penn. Historical Society, $2,500 each.

The first part of the catalogue of the library, representing, it is supposed, about one-third of the whole collection, was promptly forwarded to the society. This catalogue, prepared by J. Hammond Trumbull, LL.D., Secretary of Foreign Correspondence of the American Antiquarian Society, is a volume of 306 pages, including over 2,600 titles, and, with the instructive notes added by the compiler, is a valuable addition to bibliographical literature.

The sale began at the rooms of Geo. A. Leavitt & Co., Clinton Hall, New York, on Monday, March 10, and continued through the week, attracting a large number of gentlemen connected with the public libraries of the country, as well as many noted individual collectors. The sale was conducted by Joseph Sabin, the veteran bookseller of Nassau street, New York.

Mr. Nathaniel Paine, the Treasurer, and Mr. Edmund M. Barton, the Assistant-Librarian, were deputed to attend the sale in behalf of the Antiquarian Society.

The additions to the library made from this source consisted of two hundred and twenty-seven books and four hundred and fifty-nine pamphlets; the latter bound in convenient size, and arranged according to subjects.

The titles given in the following list are taken from the catalogue, but are arranged in chronological instead of alphabetical order. The works of the Mathers are given by themselves after the list of general titles. Nearly all of the publications of the Mathers are handsomely bound by Bedford, Pratt, and other noted binders.

LIST OF PURCHASES.

Lactantius (L. C. F.) Divinarum Institutionum Libri VII. *etc., old stamped leather on thick oak boards, clasps, large, well preserved copy.* 4° *Basileæ, Andr. Cratander.* 1521.

A scarce edition. *Title, within curious wood-cut border.* Autographs (and MSS. notes on fly-leaf) of *Increase* and *Samuel Mather.*

Mardochai, Nathan. *Meir Netib.* Concordantiarvm Hebraicarvm Capita: translata per Ant. Reuchlinum Isnensem, *old calf,* folio.
Basileæ, Henr. Petri, [1556.]

Autograph, "Crescentii Matheri Liber, London, 1691."

Bullinger. Sermonvm Decades Qvinqve, de Potissimis Christ. Religionis Capitibvs, Authore Heinricho Bullingero. Tomi III. *in one volume,* (42) and 496 *ff.* 8° *Londini, Henr. Midletonus,* [1584.]

Autogr. "*Crescentius Matherus,*" "*S. Matheri* 1720," and MSS. notes. The first English edition of Bullinger's *Decades* in Latin.

Ainsworth (Henry). An Animadversion to Mr. Richard Clyfton's Advertisement, [Wherein] the true causes of the lamentable Breach that hath lately fallen out in the English exiled Church at Amsterdam [are] manifested, *pp. (8),* 138. 4° *Amsterdam, Giles Thorp,* 1613.

From the Mather library. Autograph of Increase Mather, "Crescentii Matheri Liber ex douo Thomæ Schermandini, Londini, 1691."

Adam (Melchior). Vitæ German Orum. Theologorum, ad annum usque. 1618.
deductæ, *old calf.* thk. 8° *Haidelbergæ,* 1620.

Autogr. of Dr. *Samuel Mather,* on title, and a note in the hand of *Richard Mather,* on guard-leaf.

Las Casas. Tyrannies et Crvavtez des Espagnols commises es Indes Occidentales, . . . traduitte en François par Iacques de Miggrode, *title in red and black, pp.* (22), 214. sm. 4° *Rouen, J. Cailloue',* 1630.

Ames (Wm.) Anti-Synodalia Scripta, vel Animadversiones in Dogmatica illa, quæ Remonstrantes in Synodo Dordracena exhibuerunt, sm. 12° *Amstelodami, J. Jansson,* 1633.

Herodiani Historiæ sui Temporis libri VIII. In Linguam Latinam conversæ ab Ang. Politiano; ed. Dan. Pareus, etc., *calf.*
8° *Londini, Th. Harper,* 1639.

"*Cottonus Matherus*" (autogr.) on title and on p. 30, and a few MSS. notes.

Cotton (John). Gods Mercie mixed with his Ivstice, or, His People's Deliverance in times of danger, laid open in severell Sermous, *pp.* (8), 135, 4° *London,* 1641.

Cotton (John). A Modest and Cleare Answer to Mr. Ball's Discourse of Set Formes of Prayer, *pp.* (4), 49, (1),
4° *London, R. O. & G. D. for H. Overton,* 1642.

Another edition, 8° *London, for H. Overton,* n. d. (2 vols.)

Rogers (Nathaniel) *of Ipswich.* A Letter discovering the Cause of God's continuing Wrath against the Nation, Directing To the Meanes of appeasing that wrath, Written By Mr. Nathaniel Rogers, a godly and Learned Divine now in New-England, To a Worthy member of the House of Commons, Dec. 17, 1643 *pp.* (2), 10,
4° *London,* 1644.

Essex Witches. A true and exact Relation Of the Severall Informations, Examinations, and Confessions of the late Witches, executed in the County of Essex [England], arraigned and condemned at Chelmesford, 29 of July, 1645. Published by Authoritie, *pp.* (8), 36, sm. 4° *London, M. S. for Henry Overton and Benj. Allen,* 1645.

A Word to Mr. Peters, and Two Words for the Parliament and Kingdom; or, An Answer to a Scandalous Pamphlet entituled "A Word for the Armie," *etc.*, subscribed by Hugh Peters, *pp.* 3–38,
8° *London,* 1647.

This reply has been attributed to the Rev. Nathaniel Ward, author of "The Simple Cobler." See J. W. Dean's *Memoir of N. Ward,* pp. 174–5.

Usher (J.) Annales Veteris Testamenti. folio, *Londini,* 1650.
Autographs of *I. Mather* and *Samuel Mather,* 1723.

Whitfield (Henry). The Light appearing more and more towards the perfect Day. Or, A farther Discovery of the present state of the Indians in New-England, Concerning the Progresse of the Gospel amongst them. Manifested by Letters from such as preacht to them there. Published by Henry Whitfeld *(so),* late Pastor to the Chuch *(so)* of Christ at Gilford, *pp.* 46,
sm. 4° *London, T. R. & E. M. for John Bartlett,* 1651.

Ames (Wm.) Medulla Theologica. Editio 2da. *Amstelod.* 1628.—*The same,* Editio 4ta [Liber I.] *Lond.,* 1630.—*The same,* Editio novissima, orationibus duabus auctior. *Amst., J. Jansson,* 1652.
3 vols. 8° and 12°

Strength out of Weaknesse; Or a Glorious Manifestation Of the further Progresse of the Gospel among the Indians in Nevv-England. Held forth in Sundry Letters since the last Treatise to that effect, formerly set forth by Mr. *Henry Whitfield,* late Pastor of Gilford in New-England. Published by the aforesaid Corporation. *pp.* (12), 40.
4° *London, M. Simmons, &c.,* 1652.

The *Second* issue. *The Epistle Dedicatorie* is subscribed by *William Steele,* President (of the Corporation).

Baxter (Richard). Gildas Salvianus; The Reformed Pastor. *With the autographs of Thos. Shepard, Thos. Prince (1706), Sam. Greenwood (1707), Rich. Salter (1742), and James G. Percival.*
8° *London,* 1656.

Buxtorfi (J.) *Fil.* Exercitationes ad Historiam, I. Arcæ Fœderis, II. Ignis Sacri et Cœlestis, III. Urim et Thummim, IV. Mannæ, *etc.,* old *calf.* 4° *Basileæ,* 1659.
Autogr. "*Cottoni Matheri Liber,* 1683."

Peters (Hugh). A Sermon by Hugh Peters: preached before his Death: As it was taken by a faithful hand. *Portrait (satirical) of Peters inserted, pp. (4),* 28. *Lond., John Best,* 1660.

Leigh (Edw.) A Systeme or Body of Divinity. 2d edition.
4° *fol. London,* 1662.

Autographs of *Increase, Cotton,* and *Samuel Mather;* several marginal *notes by Increase Mather.*

Propositions concerning the subject of Baptism, *etc.,* Whereunto is annext the Answer of the Dissenting Brethren, &c.
4° n. p. *Printed in the Year,* 1662.

Torrey (Samuel). An Exhortation unto Reformation. Massachusetts Election Sermon, May 27, 1674, *pp. (8),* 44.
4° *Cambridge, Marmaduke Johnson,* 1674.

Autograph, at head of title-page, of "John Cotton ex dono Amici Grindalli Rawson." Address To the Reader (6 pp.) by Increase Mather.

Glanvil (J.) Essays on several Important Subjects, *good copy, old binding.* 4° *London,* 1676.

The Sixth Essay is against Witchcraft. SCARCE.

Owen (John). An Enquiry into the Original, Nature, *etc.,* of Evangelical Churches. The First Part; with an Answer to the Discourse on the Unreasonableness of Separation by Dr. Edward Stillingfleet, and Vindication of the Non-Conformists from the guilt of Schisme, *pp. (14),* 365. 4° *London,* 1681.

[Willard (S.)] Covenant Keeping the Way to Blessedness, in several sermons; with a Preface by I. Mather.
12° [*Boston, J. Glen for S. Sewall,* 1682.]

Oakes (Urian), *Præsident of Harvard Colledge.* A Seasonable Discourse Wherein Sincerity & Delight in the Service of God is earnestly pressed upon Professors of Religion. Delivered on a Publick Fast, at Cambridge, *pp. (6),* 23, 4° *Cambridge, Samuel Green,* 1682.

Willard (S.) The Child's Portion : Or the Unseen Glory of the Children of God, Together with several other Sermons, *pp. (6),* 227.
8° *Boston, Samuel Green,* 1684.

Contains The Child's Portion, *pp.* 144; The Righteous Man's Death (Fun. Sermon for Major Tho. Savage), *pp. (2).* 145-163; ELECTION SERMON, 1682, *pp.* 163-198; All Plots Against God and his People Detected and Defeated, Fast Sermon, Jan. 25, 1682, *pp.* 199-227.

Stoddard (Solomon). The Safety of Appearing at the Day of Judgement, in the Righteousness of Christ, *pp. (8),* 352, *(2).*
8° *Boston, S. Green, for Sam. Phillips,* 1687.

The last leaf contains a list of "Books to be Sold by Samuel Phillips, at the West end of the Town-House in Boston."

Palmer (John). An Impartial Account of the State of New England : or, the Late Government there, Vindicated. In Answer to the Declaration which the Faction set forth when they Overturned that Government. With a Relation of the Horrible Usage they treated the Governour with, and his Council, &c.; in a Letter to the Clergy there, *pp.* 49. 4° *London, for Edw. Poole,* 1690.

Willard (S.) The Mourners Cordial against Excessive Sorrow, *etc., pp. (4),* 137. 8° *Boston, B. Harris & John Allen;*
"*very suitable to be given at Funerals,*" 1691.

Judgment (The) of Several Eminent Divines of the Congregational Way, concerning a Pastor's Power Occasionally to exert Ministerial Acts in another Church, besides that which is His Own Particular Flock, *pp. (2),* 13. 8° *Boston, Benj. Harris,* 1693.

"Drawn up by Mr. Increase Mather."—*Prince.*

Moodey (Joshua). *posthumous.* The Believers happy change by Dying, A Sermon preached on the occasion of the Death of Capt. Thomas Daniel Esq., who was interred the day before, November 17th, 1683, *pp.* 32, sm. sq. 8° *Boston, B. Green and J. Allen,* 1697.

Lee (Samuel). Contemplations on Mortality. Wherein The Terrors of Death are laid open, for a Warning to Sinners; *etc., pp. (10),* 149.
8° *Boston, B. Green & J. Allen, for S. Phillips,* 1698.

Autographs of Jeremiah Dummer and Benjamin Wadsworth (President of Harvard College).

Willard (S.) The Man of War. A Sermon preached to the Artillery Company at Boston, June 5, 1699, Being the anniversary day for their Election, *pp.* 30. 8° *B. Green & J. Allen*, 1699.

Stubbes (Henry). Conscience the Best Friend upon Earth, *pp. (20)*, 64. sm. 12° *Boston, Reprinted, B. Green & J. Allen*, 1700.

Boston—Several Rules, Orders, and By-Laws made and agreed upon by the Free-Holders and Inhabitants of Boston of the Massachusetts, At their Meeting May 12 and Sept. 22, 1701; [with Rules and Orders adopted at various subsequent dates, to 1727, *paged continuously*] *pp.* 43. 4° *Boston, B. Green & J. Allen*, 1702.

Stoddard (Sol.) The Way for a People to Live Long in the Land that God Hath given them. [Election] Sermon, 26. of May, 1703. *pp. (2)*, 25. 4° *Boston, B. Green & J. Allen*, 1703.

Lawson (Deodat). Christ's Fidelity the only Shield against Satan's Malignity. A [Lecture] Sermon at Salem-Village, the 24th of March, 1692—a time of Publick Examination of some Suspected for Witchcraft. The Second Edition, *pp. (12)* 120. 8° *Reprinted, London, R. Tookey*, 1704.

This edition has a special Dedication to Sir Henry and Lady Diana Ashurst; and an Appendix (pp. 93-120) containing "Remarkable things relating to the Afflicted"—"to the accused"—and "to the Confessing Witches."

Boone (Nicholas). Military Discipline. The Compleat Soldier—Added, The Military Law of the Province. The Second Edition with Additions, *pp. (4)*, 124. 8° *Boston, B. Green for Benj. Eliot*, 1706.

The Military Laws have a separate title-page (p. 86.)

Willard (S.) The Just Man's Prerogative; A Sermon [Occasioned by the Death of] Simeon Stoddard, who was Barbarously Murdered, near London, May 14, 1706.—WADSWORTH (Benj.) Considerations to Prevent Murmuring—A Lecture Sermon [on the same occasion]. *Two in one vol.* 12° *Boston, B. Green*, 1706.

Contains MSS. biographical notes [by Samuel G. Drake.]

Williams (Wm.) The Danger of Not Reforming Known Evils, or, The Inexcusableness of a Knowing People Refusing to be Reformed. As it was set forth on a day of Publick Fasting, April 16, 1707, at Hatfield, *pp. (2)*, 30. 8° *Boston, B. Green*, 1707.

His first published sermon.

Pierpont (Rev. James). Sundry False Hopes of Heaven, Discovered and Decryed. In a Sermon in Boston, 3d. 4 m. 1711. With a Preface by the Rd. Dr. [Cotton] Mather, *pp. (2)*, XXIV. 46. 12° *Boston, T. Green*, 1712.

[Kirkpatrick (James)]. An Historical Essay upon the Loyalty of Presbyterians in Gr. Britain and Ireland from the Reformation to 1713. In Three Parts, *pp.* xvi, 564, (10). 4° *(Edinburgh)* 1713.

Mayhew (Experience). A Discourse showing that God dealeth with Men as with Reasonable Creatures. Sermon at Boston, Nov. 23, 1718. With a brief account of the State of the Indians on Martha's Vineyard, & the Small Islands Adjacent, from 1694 to 1720, *pp. (2)*, 34,12. 8° *Boston, B. Green, for S. Gerrish*, 1720.

2

Bacqueville de la Potherie. Histoire de l'Amerique Septentrionale, *plates*, 4 vols. 12° *Paris*, 1722.

This work is, chiefly, a history of the Indian nations of Canada, particularly the Iroquois, Abnakis, Hurons, and Illinois; and of the relations between these Indians and the French. Most of the twenty-seven plates are illustrative of scenes or peculiarities in Indian life.— *Field's* Bibliography, No. 66.

Stoddard (Solomon). Question whether God is not Angry with the Country for doing so little towards the Conversion of the Indians? Spoken to, in a Discourse [at] North-Hampton, *pp.* 22.
4° *Boston*, 1723.

Loring (*Rev.* Israel) *of Sudbury.* Two sermons at Rutland, Sept. 8th, 1723, After the Indians had been there and Kill'd the Rev. Joseph Willard, with Two of Mr. Joseph Stevens's Children and Captivated other Two, *pp.* (2), 44. 16° *Boston, S. Kneeland*, 1724.

York. Moodey (Samuel). Summary account of the Life and Death of Joseph Quasson, Indian; who [was Executed for Murder at York, June 29, 1726], *wanting pp.* 29-36. 16° *Boston, for S. Gerrish*, 1726.

The *narrative* part of this VERY RARE tract is complete. The missing signature contains a portion of the author's " Observations and special remarks."

Mayhew (Experience). Indian Converts : or, Some Account of the Lives and Dying Speeches of Christianized Indians of Martha's Vineyard. Added, Some Account of the English Ministers who have presided over the Indian Work, by Mr. Prince, *old paneled calf.*
8° *London, for Sam. Gerrish, Boston*, 1727.

On a guard-leaf, in the autograph of a former possessor—whose signature is illegible—the inscription : " Ex Dono Amici Integerrimi *Samuelis Matheri.*" A.M. V.D.M. Bostoni Nov-Angliæ, July 16, 1782, *Cottoni Mather* Filius, *Increase Mather* Nepos, Amici mei . . . honorandi & colendi."

Chauncey (Isaac). Sermon at the Funeral of the Rev. Mr. John Williams, Pastor of the Church in Deerfield, *pp.* 82. 8° *Boston*, 1729.

A Conference of His Excellency Jonathan Belcher, Esq. ; . . . Governor . . of the Massachusetts Bay, *etc.*, with Edewakenk Chief Sachem of the Penobscut Tribe, [and others,] at Falmouth, in Casco-Bay, July, 1732, *pp.* 23. 4° [*Boston, B. Green*, 1732.]

Plymouth Company. (Kennebec Purchase.) A defence of the Remarks of the Plymouth Company, on the Plans and Extracts of Deeds published by the Proprietors (as they term themselves) of the Township of Brunswick, *pp.* 50. 4° 1753.

Hopkins (Samuel). Historical Memoirs Relating to the Housatunnuk Indians. 4° *Boston*, 1753.

Militia. The Exercise for the Militia of the Province of the Massachusetts-Bay. fol., 1758.

Observations on Several Acts of Parliament, . and also on the Conduct of the Officers of the Customs, since those Acts were passed . . Published by the Merchants of Boston. *Edes & Gill*, 1769.—State of the Importations from Great Britain into the port of Boston, Jan.-Aug., 1769, &c., *pp.* 130, *Mein & Fleming*, 1769.

Boston. [Adams (Sam.)] Appeal to the World; or, a Vindication of the Town of Boston, 8° *Boston*, 1769.

Massacre. A Short Narrative of The horrid Massacre in Boston, perpetrated in the Evening of the Fifth Day of March, 1770, by Soldiers of the xxixth Regiment; . . with some Observations on the State of Things prior to that Catastrophe, *frontispiece (inserted).*
8° *Printed by Order of the Town of Boston,* 1770.

Gordon (*Rev.* Wm.) Plan of a Society for making Provision for Widows by Annuities. 8° 1772.

Mauduit (I.) Short View of the History of the Colony of Massachusetts Bay, with respect to their Charters and Constitution, *half mor.*
8° London, 1774.

Letters of Governor Hutchinson and Lieut. Gov. Oliver, &c., printed at Boston, and Remarks thereon; with the Assembly's Address, and the Proceedings of the Lords Committee of Council, *pp.* 126, *half morocco.*
8° London, 1774.

Emmons William. Address in Commemoration of the Boston Massacre. Calculated for the Northern but will answer all Southern tastes. 2d Edition, pp. 14. n. d.
In same volume is "Some Strictures upon the Sacred Story of Esther, etc." By Oliver Noble, pp. 31. Newburyport, 1775.

Hanson (Eliz.) An Account of the Captivity of Elizabeth Hanson, late of Kachecky in New England: Who, with four of her children and Servant-Maid, was taken Captive by the Indians, and carried into Canada. . . . A New Edition. Taken in substance, from her own Mouth by Samuel Bownas. 8° *London,* 1787.

[Trumbull (Henry)]. History of the Discovery of America, *etc.*, and of . . . Engagements with the Indians . . . By a Citizen of Connecticut, *two folded plates, pp.* 184.
8° *Norwich, for the Author at his Office,* 1810.

Greene (Nathanael). Life and Correspondence, by William Johnson. 2 vols., *portraits, maps, and plans, uncut.* 4° *Charleston,* 1822.

Captivities. Narrative of the Captivity of Mrs. Johnson. With an Appendix containing the Sermons preached at her Funeral, and that of her Mother. *etc.* Third Edition, enlarged. *pp.* 178, *the first few leaves worn. and water stained. Windsor, Vt.,* 1814.—Good fetch'd out of Evil, in Three Short Essays. I. A Pastoral Letter of Mr. John Williams, of Deerfield; now detain'd a captive in Canada, *etc.* II. The conduct and constancy of the New English Captives, when strongly tempted unto Popish Idolatries, *etc.* III. An account of memorable deliverances, *etc., pp.* 34. *n. p.* 1784.—Narrative of Remarkable occurrences in the Life of John Blatchford, of Cape-Ann, Commonwealth of Massachusetts, Containing an Account of his treatment and sufferings while a prisoner in the late War, *etc.* Second Edition, *pp.* 22. *New London, Timothy Green,* 1794.—Williams (Stephen W.) Biographical Memoir of the Rev. John Williams [the "Redeemed Captive"]; with a Sketch of Ancient Deerfield; the Journal of the Rev. Dr. Stephen Williams of Longmeadow, during his Captivity, *etc., pp.* 127. *Greenfield, Mass.,* 1837.—Narrative of the Captivity etc. of Mrs. Mary Rowlandson, *pp.* 122. *Boston,* 1856.—Memoirs of Rev. Joseph Eastburn, of the Mariner's Church, Philadelphia. By Ashbel Green, D.D. [With an Appendix, containing] A Faithful Narrative of the many Dangers &c. of Robert Eastburn during his Captivity among the Indians, &c. [repr. from Philadelphia edition of 1758]. *Portrait, pp.* vi, 208, *Phila.* 1828. *Six volumes and tracts, bound in one vol.* 12°

The History of the Province of Massachusetts Bay, from 1750 until June, 1774. Edited by the Rev. John Hutchinson. 3 vols.
8° *London, J. Murray*, 1828.

Bouchette (Jos.) The British Dominions in North America : or, a Topographical and Statistical Description of Lower and Upper Canada, New Brunswick, Nova Scotia, *etc.*, 33 *plates*, 2 vols. 4° *London*, 1831.

The Witches; a Tale of New-England, *curious woodcuts, pp. 72.*
18° *Bath (Me.), R. L. Underhill*, 1837.

New Haven. Yale College. Tracts. 17 *in one vol.*
New Haven (except two), 1768-95.

Swett (S.) History of the Battle of Bunker Hill. 2d edition with a plan, 1826. Swett (S.) Notes to his Sketch, 1825. Précis historique sur la Bataille, pour servir d'explication du Tableau peint par le Col. Trumbull, *London*, 1786. Bradford (A.) History of the Battle, 1825. 5 in one vol. Report to Mass. Legislature on Monument to Col. Prescott, 1852. 8°

Phinney (E.) History of the Battle at Lexington, 1825. Ripley (E.) History of the Fight at Concord, *Concord*, 1827. Everett (E.) Hist. Address at Lexington, Apr. 19, 1835, 2d ed., *Charlestown*, 1835. King (D. P.) Address at Danvers, commemor. of Seven Young Men slain in the Battle of Lexington, *Salem*, 1835. Emmons (W.) Address in Commem. of Lexington Battle, 1826. Everett (E.) Oration at Concord, April 19, 1825. Celebration at Concord, Apr. 19, 1850, with Oration by R. Rantoul, Jun., *pp.* 135. *Boston*, 1850. 7 *in one vol.* 8°

Bartlett (J. R.) History of the Destruction of the Gaspee, in Narragansett Bay, June 10, 1772, *Providence*, 1861. Dring (T.) Recollections of the *Jersey* Prison-Ship; edited by H. B. Dawson, *(25 copies printed) two portraits, Morrisania*, 1865. 2 *in* 1 *vol.,* royal 8°

Lescarbot (Marc). Histoire de la Nouvelle-France; Suivie des Muses de la Nouvelle-France. Nouvelle Edition, publiée par E. Tross, avec *quatre cartes* géographiques, 3 vols.,
8° *Paris, Libraire Tross*, 1866.
Literal reprint of the edition of 1612, with facsimiles of the maps.

Drake (S. G.) Annals of Witchcraft in New England and elsewhere in the U. States, *pp.* 306, *portrait of Hon. John Wentworth.*
4° *Boston*, 1869.
No. VIII. of Woodward's *Historical Series;* edition of 250 copies.

Whitmore (W. H.) Increase Mather, the Agent of Massachusetts Colony in England, for the Concession of a Charter. Reprinted from the "Andros Tracts." *pp.* 24, *uncut.* sm. 4° *Boston*, 1869.

Harvard College Tracts. 46 in 3 vols. 8°

Plymouth Tracts. 59 in 3 vols. 8°

American Revolution—Tracts. 1768-1774.

American Indians —Tracts. Wars and Captivities.

WORKS OF THE MATHERS.

Mather (Richard). A Defence of the Answer and Arguments of the Synod met at Boston in the year 1662, concerning the Subject of Baptism and Consociation of Churches against the Reply made thereto by the Reverend John Davenport—Together with An Answer [by the Rev. Jonathan Mitchell] to the Apologetical Preface set before that Essay. By some of the Elders who were members of that Synod, *pp. (2), 46, 102.* 4° *Cambridge.*

On the margin of the title-page, is written, in the Autograph of Richard Mather: "For the Reverd Mr. Shepard;" also, "Thomas Shepard's Booke, ye gift of ye Revd. Author [Mr. Richard] Mather, Teacher of the Church in Dorchester;" and "Ben. Wadsworth's, 1717."

[Mather (Increase? and Nathanael)]. A Disputation Concerning Church Members and their Children, in Answer to XXI. Questions: Wherein the State of Such Children when Adults, Together with their Duty towards the Church, And the Churches Duty towards them is Discussed. By an Assembly of Divines meeting at Boston in New England, June 4th, 1657. *pp. 8, 31.* 4° *London, J. Hayes, for Samuel Thomson,* 1659.

This VERY RARE tract was published by the agency of *Nathaniel* and *Increase* Mather. The former wrote the prefatory Epistle "To the Reader."

INCREASE MATHER.

The Mystery of Israel's Salvation Explained and Applyed, Or, A Discourse concerning the general Conversion of the Israelitish Nation. By Increase Mather M. A., Teacher of a Church in Boston in New England, *pp. (46), 181, (10).* 8° n. p. [*London?*] *Printed in the year* 1669.

A Second title-page, placed after the Preface, has the Imprint: *London, Printed for John Allen in Wentworth Street, near Bell Lane,* 1669.

This is the FIRST of Increase Mather's acknowledged publications.

Collation: Epistle to the Reader, by John Davenport, 1667 (11 pp.); To the Reader, by W. G. (4 pp.); To the Reader, by W. H[ooke] (14 pp.); The Author's Preface (14 pp.); Text, pp. 181; Table, &c., (9 pp.)

Wo to Drunkards. Two Sermons testifying against the Sin of Drunkenness. 4° *Cambridge, Marmaduke Johnson,* 1673.

Pray for the Rising Generation, or a Sermon Wherein Godly Parents are Encouraged, to Pray and Believe for their Children, Preached [on a Fast in Boston, July 3, 1678], *pp. 28.* 4° *Cambridge, Samuel Green,* 1678.

Returning unto God, the Great Concernment of a Covenant People. Or a Sermon Preached to the second Church in Boston, March 17, 1679-80, [on their Renewal of their Covenant.] *pp. (6), 18, (2).* 4° *John Foster,* 1680.

Title leaf (2 pp.); To the Second Church (4 pp.); Sermon, pp. 19; The Covenant (2 pp.) At the end, a manuscript note, by Thomas Prince; "*I have the 1st rough draught of this Covenant, drawn by Mr. Increase Mather in his own Hand-writing. T. Prince.*"

Heaven's Alarm to the World. Or a Sermon, wherein it is shewed, That Fearful Sights and Signs in Heaven, are the Presages of great Calamities at hand. *pp.* 6, 17. 4° *John Foster,* 1681.

An Essay for the Recording of Illustrious Providences: especially in New England. *pp. (22), 372 (8). sm. 8°. Printed at Boston in New-England, and are to be sold by George Calvert, at the Sign of the Half-Moon, in Paul's Church-yard, London,* 1684.

The Mystery of Christ opened and applyed. In several Sermons. *pp. (2),* 6, 212. *Boston,* 8° 1686.

A Sermon Occasioned by the Execution of a Man found Guilty of Murder. Preached at Boston in New England, March 11, 1685-6. Together with the Confession, Last Expressions and Solemn Warning of that Murderer, &c., *pp. (4),* 44.
8° *Printed for Joseph Brunning,* 1686.

The FIRST Edition. Sibley (No. 39) notes only the *Second* edition of 1687. Bound in the same volume, are the following tracts:

Yearwood (Randolph). The Penitent Murderer. An Exact Narrative of the Life and Death of Nathaniel Butler [who murdered] John Knight, with the several Confessions held with the said Butler in *Newgate,* &c. *London, T. Newcomb,* 1657.

Mather (Cotton). The Call of the Gospel Applyed to all Men in general, and unto a Condemned Malefactor in particular, in A Sermon preached on the 7th d. of the 1st m. 1686, at the Request and in the hearing of a man [James Morgan] under a just Sentence of Death for the horrid Sin of Murder. *Boston, R. P[ierce],* 1686.

[This is the *First* work named in Samuel Mather's list of his Father's publications.]

Moody (Joshua). An Exhortation to a Condemned Malefactor, Delivered March 7th, 1685-6. *Boston, [R. Pierce],* 1686.

Four in 1 *vol.*

A Sermon Occasioned by the Execution of a Man found Guilty of Murder, etc., *pp.* 32. *London, for John Dunton,* 1691. [Appended to] The Wonders of Free Grace, Or, A Compleat History of the Remarkable Penitents that have been executed at Tyburn and elsewhere for these last thirty years. *pp. (8),* 180. *sm.* 8° *London,* 1690.

De Successu Evangelii apud INDOS Occidentales, in Novâ-Angliâ; Epistola. Ad Cl. Virum D. Johannem Leusdenum A Crescentio Mathero, *pp.* 16. 8° *Ultrajecti, apud Wilh. Broedeleth,* 1699.

Reprinted from the (first) London edition ("Typis J. G." 1688) and "Successu Evangelii apud Indos *Orientales* aucta."

Ichabod. Or, A Discourse, shewing what Cause there is to Fear that the Glory of the Lord, is departing from New-England. Delivered in Two Sermons, *pp.* 92. 12° *Timothy Green,* 1702.

Four Sermons, viz., I. The Glorious Throne. II. The Excellency of a Public Spirit. III. The Righteous Man a Blessing. IV. The Morning Star. *pp. (2),* 97-122, 84. 12° *Printed for N. Boone,* 1708.

"The Glorious Throne," which has a separate title-page, was printed in 1702, appended to "Ichabod." The other three sermons were published together, in 1702. This copy has the autograph of Rev. Thomas Foxcroft, "*Don. Autoris venerabilis. Jan. 8, 1722-3.*"

A Discourse concerning Faith and Fervency in Prayer Several Sermons with a True Account of the late Wonderful and Astonishing

Success of the Gospel in Ceilon, Amboina, and Malabar, *pp. (2)*, xix, *(1)*, 112, *(6)*, *wants a leaf of preface.*
12° *B. Green for Samuel Gerrish*, 1710.

A Discourse concerning the Death of the Righteous. Occasioned by the Death of the Honourable Mr. John Foster, Esqr., and of his Pious Consort, Mrs. Abigail Foster, *pp. (2)*, 29. 8° *B. Green*, 1711.

Now or Never is the Time for Men to make Sure of their Eternal Salvation. Several Sermons, *pp. (4)*, 113. 12° *T. Green*, 1713.

A Sermon concerning Obedience & [Resignation] to the Will of God. Occasion'd by the Death of that Pious Gentlewoman Mrs. Mari[ah Mather,] late consort of Increase Mather, D.D. on the Lord's Day, April 4, 1714, *pp. (2)*, vi, 40. 12° *T. Green*, 1714.

A Discourse concerning the Existence and Omniscience of God, The Substance of several Sermons, *pp. (6)*, 86, *(1)*. 12° [1716.]
The Preface is dated, Oct. 10, 1716.

Two Discourses shewing I. That the Lord's Ears are open to the Prayers of the Righteous. II. The Dignity & Duty of Aged Servants of the Lord. Also, A Preface in which the Congregational Discipline of the Churches in New-England is Vindicated, with the Author's Dying Testimony there-unto, *pp. (2)*, x, 141, *(1)*, *old binding.*
12° *B. Green, for D. Henchman*, 1716.

The Preface (pp. ix.) is dated July 26, 1716. "Nine and Fifty Years are Lapsed, since I began to Preach the Gospel, in my Youth, in lands afar off. Since God brought me to Boston, Five and Fifty Years are within a few Weeks expired. What Changes have I lived to see!"

The Duty of Parents to Pray for their Children. A Sermon, preached May 19, 1703. [on a Day of] Prayer with Fasting for the Rising Generation. The Second Impression, *pp. vi, 40.*—Mather (Cotton) The Duty of Children Whose Parents have Pray'd for them. Or, Early and Real Godliness Urged; Especially upon such as are descended from Godly Ancestors. A Sermon [on the same occasion as the preceding.] The Second Impression, *pp.* 41-99. *Two in one volume, continuous paging.* 12° *J. Allen, for John Edwards*, 1719.

Awakening Soul-Saving Truths, Plainly Delivered in several Sermons [on the Called and the Chosen], *pp. (2)*, *ii.*, 100, *(1)*.
12° *S. Kneeland, for B. Gray and J. Edwards*, 1720.

Sermon on the Beatitudes. The Second Edition, *pp. (6)*, 211.
Reprinted, Dublin, 1721.

With it are bound: BOYSE (J.) Sermon on the Accession of George I. *Dublin*, 1715; and BURKITT (W.) Discourses of Infant Baptism. *Lond.* 1712.

A Dying Legacy of a Minister to his Dearly Beloved People, Being the THREE LAST SERMONS preached by him. (Preface, dated June 21st, 1722,) *pp. (6)*, 90. sm. 12° 1722.

The Original Rights of Mankind Freely to Subdue and Improve the Earth. Asserted and Maintained. By I. [or J.] M. *pp. (6)*, 22. UNCUT
8° *Boston, for the Author*, 1722.

Attributed to I. Mather, which may not be correct. If by him it is the last work independently published by him.

COTTON MATHER.

Small Offers towards the Service of the Tabernacle in the Wilderness. Four Discourses accommodated unto the Designs of Practical Godliness. *Wants pp. 23-4 and 45-6 (two leaves) otherwise perfect.*
8° *R. Pierce*, 1689.

Several Sermons concerning Walking with God, and that In the Dayes of Youth, *pp.* (2), 86. 8° *London, J. Astwood for John Dunton*, 1689.
Three Sermons. The last is entitled, "The Duty and Interest of Youth: or, The Thought of an Elder, on the Death of a Younger Brother, Uttered Oct. 28, 1688"(a funeral sermon for Nathanael Mather).

Late Memorable Providences Relating to Witchcrafts and Possessions, Clearly Manifesting, Not only that there are Witches but that Good Men (as well as others) may possibly have their Lives shortned by such evil Instruments of Satan. The Second Impression. Recommended by the Reverend Mr. Richard Baxter in London, and by the Ministers of Boston and Charlestown in New-England. *pp.* (22), 144. 8° *London, Tho. Parkhurst*, 1691.
One of the EARLIEST and RAREST American works relating to the subject.

Batteries upon the Kingdom of the Devil. Seasonable Discourses upon Some Common, but Woful, Instances, wherein Men Gratifie the Grand Enemy of their Salvation. By Mr. Cotton Mather, *Author* of The Late Memorable Providences relating to Witchcrafts and Possessions, *and of* Early Piety exemplified, *pp.* (16,) 192.
8° *London, Nath. Hiller*, 1695.
An Epistle Dedicatory, "To my Worthy Nephew, Mr. Cotton Mather," and an address "To the Reader." by Nath. Mather,—the former, dated, London, Dec. 15, 1693. The first sermon in the volume, "Sacred Exorcisms: Or. The Case and Cure of Persons Possessed by the Devil," alludes (p. 21) to cases "we have seen," of "bodily molestations by Evil Spirits."

Benedictus. Good men described, with some Character and History of Mr. Thomas Bridge. 1715. *Bound with* The Best Ornaments of Youth, *etc.*

The Thoughts of a Dying Man. A Faithful Report of Matters uttered by many, in the Last Minutes of their Lives, *etc.*, *pp.* 47, (1), *four pages* (17-20) *in admirable fac-simile, by Burt.*
12° *B. Green & J. Allen, for J. Wheeler*, 1697.

A Token for the Children of New-England. Or, Some Examples of Children in whom the Fear of God was Remarkably Budding, before they Dyed, In Several Parts of New-England . . . Added as Supplement, unto the excellent Janewayes Token for Children: Upon the Reprinting of it, in this Countrey, *pp.* 36, [Appended to Janeway's Token, *pp.* (12), 132]. 12° *Timo. Green, for B. Eliot*, 1700.

An Advice to the Churches of the Faithful; briefly reporting, The Present State of the Church, throughout the World, *pp.* 16.
8° *B. Green and J. Allen*, 1702.

A Tree Planted by the Rivers of Water. Or, An Essay, upon the Godly and Glorious Improvements, which Baptised Christians are to make of their Sacred Baptism, *pp.* (2), 69.
12° *Barth. Green, for Samuel Phillips*, 1704.

Work Within-Doors. An Essay to Assist the Serious in the Grand Exercise of Conversing with themselves, and Communing with their own Hearts, *pp.* 40. 12° *T. Green*, 1709.

    The running title is: " A Christian Conversing with himself."

The Sailours Companion and Counsellour: An Offer of Considerations for the Tribe of Zebulun; Awakening the Mariner to Think and to Do those things that may render his Voyage Prosperous, *pp.* (2), 62.
    8° *B. Green, for S. Gerrish*, 1709.

A Golden Curb, For the Mouth, which with an Headstrong Folly, Rushes into the Sins of Profane Swearing and Cursing, *pp.* 12.
    12° *John Allen*. 1709.

Orphanotrophium. Or, Orphans Well-provided for. An Essay on the Care taken in the Divine Providence for Children when their Parents forsake them. A Sermon, on a Day of Prayer, kept with a Religious Family, [28d. 1m. 1711,] whose Honourable parents [John and Abigail Foster] were lately taken from them, *pp.* (4), 68. 8° *B. Green*, 1711.

Winter Piety . . A Sermon at Boston-Lecture, 27d. 10m. 1711, *pp.* (2), 33. 12° *B. Green*, 1712.

Seasonable Thoughts upon Mortality. A Sermon occasioned by the Raging of a Mortal Sickness in the Colony of Connecticut, and the many Deaths of our Brethren there. Delivered at Boston-Lecture, 24d. 11m. 1711-12, *pp.* (2), 26, (2). 12° *T. Green*, 1712.

Reason Satisfied: and Faith Established. The Resurrection of a glorious Jesus Demonstrated, *pp.* 47. 12° *J. Allen, for N. Boone*, 1712.

Grata Brevitas. An Essay made in a Few Words, to demonstrate that a Few Words may have Much comprised in them, *pp.* 20.
    8° *B. Green, for S. Gerrish*, 1712.

Wholesome Words. A Visit of Advice, Given unto Families that are Visited with Sickness; by a Pastoral Letter, *etc. pp.* (2), 24.
    12° *Printed for D. Henchman*, 1713.

    In S. Mather's list, the title is given under 1702.

A Flying Roll, Brought forth, to Enter into the House and Hand of the Thief. The Crime and the Doom of the Thief declared. The various Wayes of Theft Detected and Exposed . . A Sermon preached at Boston, 11d. 11m. 1712, *pp.* (2), 34. 8° *B. Green*, 1713.

The Saviour with his Rainbow. A Discourse concerning the Covenant which God will remember in the Times of Danger passing over his Church. (Dedication by Samuel Mather.) *pp.* 23. 8° *London*, 1714.

The Religion of the Cross. A Brief Essay upon the Cross, . . Occasioned by . . the Death of [the author's wife] Mrs. *Elizabeth Mather*, *pp.* (4), 47, (1). 12° *John Allen*, 1714.

A New Year Well-begun. An Essay offered on A New-Years-Day; to provide a Good Work for such a Day, and Advise, How a Good Year may Certainly follow the Day, *pp.* (4), 29. 1.
    16° *New London, T. Green*, 1719.

    Dedicated to John Winthrop, Esq.

A Glorious Espousal. A Brief Essay to Illustrate and Prosecute the Marriage, wherein Our Great Saviour offers to Espouse unto Himself the Children of Men; And there upon to Recommend . . a good Car-

riage in the Married Life. An Essay . . Seasonably to be presented, where a Marriage is upon a Celebration. *pp.* (2), 46.
12° *S. Kneeland, for B. Gray,* 1719.

The World Alarm'd. A Surprizing Relation of a new Burning-Island lately raised out of the Sea near Tercera; . . and a Brief History of other Ignivomous Mountains . . In a Letter to an Honourable Fellow of the Royal Society at London, From a Member of the same Society, *pp.* 16, (2). 8° *B. Green,* 1721.

Bethiah. The Glory Which Adorns the Daughters of God. And the Piety, Wherewith Zion wishes to see her Daughters Glorious, *pp.* 60.
12° *J. Franklin, for S. Gerrish,* 1722.

Sober Sentiments. In an Essay upon the Vain Presumption of Living and Thriving in the World. . . Produced by the Premature and much lamented Death of Mr. Joshua Lamb. With an Appendix by another Hand [Rev. Thomas Walter], *pp.* 37. Sm. 8° *T. Fleet,* 1722.

Juga Jucunda. A Brief Essay to obtain from Young People, an Early and Hearty Submission to the Yoke of their Saviour, and his Religion. With a Relation of . . . the Dying Hours of Mrs. Abiel Goodwin. The Second Edition, *pp.* (4), 36. 8° *For D. Henchman,* 1728.
This copy has the leaf before the title, with a half-title: "Dr. Mather's Remarkables on the Peaceful and Joyful Death of Mrs. Abiel Goodwin;" which was the title of the first edition, printed in 1727.

Boanerges. A Short Essay to preserve and Strengthen the Good Impressions Produced by Earthquakes . . Address'd unto the Whole People of New-England, who have been Terrified with the Late Earthquakes, etc., *pp.,* 52. 8° [1727].

Student and Preacher, entituled, Manuductio ad Ministerium; or Directions for a Candidate of the Ministry; republished by John Ryland.
8° *London,* 1781.

SAMUEL MATHER.

The Figures or Types of the Old Testament . . Explained and Improved in sundry Sermons. Second edition, *pp.* vii, (1), 540, (16).
4° *London,* 1705.
The first edition was printed in 1683, n. p. [Dublin?]

The Self-Justiciary Convicted. Or, A Discourse Concerning the Difficulty and Necessity of Renouncing our own Righteousness, *etc., pp.* (2), 27, (1), 94. 8° *Boston, B. Green, for N. Porter at Windsor,* 1707.
"A Testimony to the Order of the Gospel, in the Churches of New-England," by John Higginson and Wm. Hubbard, follows the Epistle Dedicatory, pp. 19-27.

A Compendious History of the Rise and Progress of the Reformation of the Church here in England, from Popish Darkness and Superstition. Together with an Account of Nonconformity . . . Also, King Charles II's Declaration about Religion, October, 1660, *etc.* By a Gentleman, *pp.* (16), 148. 8° *London,* 1715.
"N.B. A great part of this book is (almost Verbatim) a Transcript of Dr. Cotton Mather's *Eleutheria* or History of the Reformation & Nonconformity, Printed at London, anno 1698; with some Extracts from Dr. Calamy's Abridgement. And by the Stile of the Preface, as well as upon other considerations. I guess that this Compendious History was put forth by Mr. Samuel Mather, in England, Brother to the Doctor."— *MS. note by the Rev. Thomas Foxcroft.*

A Vindication of the Holy Bible, Wherein the Arguments for, and Objections against the Divine Original, Purity, and Integrity of the Scripture, are Proposed and Considered, *pp.* (4), iv, 405, *old calf, gilt.*
8° *London*, 1723.

Dedicated to the Rev. Edm. Calamy, D.D. Dr. Samuel Mather's copy with his marginal notes.

A Testimony from the Scripture against Idolatry & Superstition, etc., *pp.* (6), 88. 8° n. d. [*Boston*, 1725.]

"Printed in 1725, according to a MS. note," in the Prince Library copy. This copy has, at the top of the title-page, the inscription, "Donum Dom. Rev'di Joh. W[ise?] 172[ ]," the last numeral having been cut off in trimming.

Vita B. Augusti Hermanni Franckii, cui adjecta est, Narratio Rerum Memorabilium in Ecclesiis Evangelicis per Germaniam, *pp.* 31, 11, *autograph of Benjamin Colman.* 8° *Bostoni*, 1733.

Mather (Nathanael) *of Dublin and London, son of Richard; (Harv. Coll. 1647).* The Righteousness of God through Faith upon All without Difference who believe. In Two Sermons on Romans 3. 22. *pp.* (4), 76. 2d Edition. 4° *London*, 1718.

PUBLICATIONS OF THE MATHERS

In preparing this list, the titles have been compared with the originals, except in a few cases where, in the copies owned by the society, the title page was missing. Free use has been made of the large list of Mather publications in Sabin's valuable "Dictionary of Books Relating to America," and of the catalogue of the first part of the Brinley Library, prepared by J. Hammond Trumbull, LL.D.

The titles are given in chronological order, beginning with the works of Richard Mather of Dorchester, who was born in England, A. D. 1596, and died in Dorchester, Mass., A. D. 1669. Those of other members of the family are arranged in the following order:—(1), Samuel of Dublin, son of Richard, 1626–1671; (2), Nathanael of Dublin and London, son of Richard, 1630–1697; (3), Eleazer of Northampton, son of Richard, 1637–1669; (4), Increase of Boston, son of Richard, 1639–1723; (5), Cotton of Boston, son of Increase, 1663–1728; (6), Azariah of Saybrook, son of Samuel, of Windsor, Conn.; (7), Samuel of Boston, son of Cotton, 1706–1785; (8), Moses of Middlesex (now Darien), Conn., Yale College, 1739.

RICHARD MATHER.

Church-Government and Church-Covenant Discvssed, In an Answer of the Elders of the severall Churches in New England To two and thirty Questions, sent over to them by divers Ministers in England, to declare their judgments therein. Together with an Apologie of the said Elders in New-England for Church-Covenant, sent over in Answer to Master Bernard in the year 1639. As also in an Answer to nine Positions about Church-Government. And now published for the satisfaction of all who desire resolution in those points. *pp.* (4), 84, (2), 78.

4° *London, Printed by R. O. and G. D. for Benjamin Allen, Anno Dom.*, 1643.

In one of the two copies of this work in the Society's library the following in the hand-writing of Increase Mather appears on a fly leaf: "My father wrote ye Answer to ye 32 Qs Increase Mather." The "Apologie" has a separate title page and paging, and is printed by T. P. and M. S. for Benjamin Allen. On the title page of the Society's copy, Mr. Richard Mather is given as the author, in the hand-writing of Increase Mather. The "Answer of the Elders" begins with page 49, and in one copy the author is stated, in the hand-writing of Increase Mather to be Mr. Richard Mather, and in the other copy also in the same hand-writing, to be John Davenport. The Society also have a manuscript transcript of the "Answer to the Nine Positions" by John Ferniside, dated 1639. There is nothing in the manuscript itself to indicate that it was not original with Ferniside, the word "transcript" being in another hand, apparently that of Increase Mather.

The Workes of Several Authors upon That Way of Church-Government commonly called (INDEPENDENT) . . . . Unto which is added the practice of primative Times for preserving Truth, and suppressing Heresie and Schisme. . . . . Licensed and Printed According to Order. 4° *London, Printed by M. S. for H. Overton,* 1646.

The first work is "A Modest & Brotherly Answer To Mr. Charles Herle his Book, against the Independency of Churches." By Richard Mather Teacher of the Church at Dorhcester; and William Thompson Pastor of the Church at. Braintree. *pp.* (4), 58, 1644.

Then follow, The Keyes of the Kingdom of Heaven, etc , by John Cotton, pp. 59, 1644. An Answer to W. R. his Narration, etc., by Thomas Welde, pp. (6), 68. A Reply to a Confutation of some grounds for Infants Baptisme, etc., by Geo. Phillips, pp. (12), 4, 154—1645. Satisfaction Concerning Mixt Communions, etc., etc. "Imprimatur John Bachiler," pp. (2), 14, 1643. A Vindication of Churches, etc., etc., by Henry Burton, pp. (4), 72, 1644. Independency accused, etc., etc., signed J. P., pp. (4), 34, 1645. A Defence of Sundry Positions, etc., etc., by Samuel Eaton, Teacher, and Timothy Taylor, Pastor, pp. (8), 130, 4, 1645. The Defence of Sundry Positions & Scriptures Justified, etc., by the same authors, pp. (4), 46, 1646. Uniformity Examined, etc., by Wil. Dell, pp. 8, 1646. Flagellum Flagelli, by J. S., pp. (1), (2), 19, 1, 1645. The Ancient Bounds, etc., pp. 1–(6), 78. A Vindication of Mr. Burroughes, etc., by Jer. Burroughes, pp. 1–30, MDCXLVI. A Paraenetick or Humble Addresse, etc. The second impression, pp. (1), 14, 1644. To The High Court of Parliament, etc., pp. (1), 5–5–1, 1646. The Primitive Practise for Preserving Truth, etc., by Sir Simonds D'Ewes, The 2d impression. pp. 1, (2), 65, 1645.

A Farewell Exhortation to the Church and People of Dorchester in New-England, *pp.* 4–27. 4° *Cambridge*, 1657.

Journal of Richard Mather, 1635. His Life and Death, 1670. In Collections of the Dorchester Antiquarian and Historical Society. Number Three: *pp.* 108. 12° *Boston*, 1850.

SAMUEL MATHER (OF DUBLIN).

The Figures or Types of the Old Testament, By which Christ and the Heavenly Things of the Gospel were Preached and Shadowed to the People of God of Old; Explain'd and Improv'd in Sundry Sermons. *pp.* (vii), 540, 12. 4° *London*, 1705.

NATHANAEL MATHER (OF DUBLIN AND LONDON).

A Sermon Wherein is Shewed That it is the Duty and should be the Care of Believers on Christ, to Live in the Constant Exercise of Grace. By Mr. Nathanael Mather, Pastor of a Church at Dublin in Ireland. *pp. (2), 28, (2).*
    Sm. 8° *Printed at Boston in New-England By R. P., for Joseph Browning, Stationer, Anno,* 1684.
    " The first work independently published by him."—*Sabin.*

A Discussion-of the Lawfulness of a Pastor's Acting as an Officer In Other Churches besides that which He is specially called to take the Oversight of. By the late Reverend Mr. Nathanael Mather. *pp. (2),* x, 83, *(1).* The Second Edition.
    12° *Boston: Re-printed and sold by Thomas Fleet in Pudding Lane,* 1730.
    There is also a manuscript copy of this with the date. " Printed for Nathl. Hiller, London, 1698." This is probably a copy from the first edition.

ELEAZER MATHER.

A Serious Exhortation to the Present and Succeeding Generation in New England, Earnestly calling upon all to Endeavour that the Lord's Gracious Presence may be continued with Posterity. being the Substance of the Last Sermons preached By Mr. Eleazer Mather, late Pastor of the Church in Northampton in New-England. *pp.* (8), 31.
    Cambridge, Printed by S. G. and M. J., 1671.

    The second edition. pp. 4, 31. 4° Boston, Printed by John Foster, 1678. The address " To the Church and Inhabitants of Northampton," (pp. 5). in the first edition and the Letter " To the Reader " pp. 2, in the second are by Increase Mather.

INCREASE MATHER.

A Discourse Concerning the Subject of Baptisme Wherein the present Controversies, that are agitated in the New English Churches are from Scripture and Reason modestly enquired into, By Increase Mather, Teacher of a Church in Boston in New-England. *pp.* (4), 76.
    4° *Cambridge, Printed by Samuel Green,* 1675.

The First Principles of New-England, Concerning The Subject of Baptisme & Communion of Churches. Collected partly out of the Printed Books, but chiefly out of the Original Manuscripts of the First and chief Fathers in the New-English Churches; With the Judgment of Sundry Learned Divines of the Congregational Way in England, Concerning the said Questions. Published for the Benefit of those who are of the Rising Generation in New-England. By Increase Mather, Teacher of a Church in Boston in New-England. *pp.* (8), 76. 4° *Cambridge, Printed by Samuel Green,* 1675.

The Wicked maus Portion. Or A Sermon (Preached at the Lecture in Boston in New England the 18th day of the I Moneth 1674, when two men were executed, who had murthered their Master.) Wherein is shewed That excesse in wickedness doth bring untimely Death. By Increase Mather, Teacher of a Church of Christ. *pp.* (4), 25.
4° *Boston, Printed by John Foster,* 1675.

"This appears to have been the first work printed in Boston. The preface is dated '15. of 2. Moneth [April 15]. 1675.' 'The Times of Men,' has the same date of imprint, but the preface is dated '9th of 4th Moneth [June 9th] 1675.' and the accident which occasioned it occurred *May 4th*, 1675. There is another issue in which two lines are added to the errata, on the last page (25), and an error in a marginal note on the same page is corrected."

A Brief History of the VVarr With the Indians in Nevv-England. (From June 24, 1675. when the first English-man was murdered by the Indians, to August 12, 1676. when *Philip* alias *Metacomet*, the principal Author and Beginner of the Warr, was slain.) Wherein the Grounds, Beginning, and Progress of the Warr, is summarily expressed. Together with a serious Exhortation to the Inhabitants of that Land. *pp.* (6), 51. (8).
4° *Boston, Printed and Sold by John Foster over against the Sign of the Dove,* 1676.

A Call from Heaven To the Present and Succeeding Generations. Or A Discourse Wherein is shewed, I. That the Children of Godly Parents are under special Advantages and Encouragements to seek the Lord. II. The exceeding danger of Apostasie. Delivered in a Sermon, Preached in the Audience of the General Assembly of the Massachusetts Colony, at Boston in New-England, May 23. 1677. being the day of Election there. III. That Young Men ought to Remember God their Creator. *pp.* (6), 114,
Sm. 8° *Boston: Printed by John Foster,* 1679.

Also The Second Impression. 8° *pp.* (8), 198. *Boston: Printed by R. P. for I. Brunning.* 1685.

Pray for the Rising Generation, Or A Sermon Wherein Godly Parents are Encouraged to Pray and Believe for their Children, Preached the third Day of the fifth Moneth, 1678, which Day was set apart by the second Church in Boston in New-England, humbly to seek unto God by Fasting and Prayer, for a Spirit of Converting Grace, to be poured out upon the Children and Rising Generation in New England. By Increase Mather, Teacher of that Church. The Second Impression. *pp.* 29.
Sm 8° *Boston: Printed by John Foster,* 1679.

Also The Third Impression Printed by R. P. 1689.

The 1st Edition of this was bought at the Brinley Sale.

The Divine Right of Infant Baptisme Asserted and Proved from Scripture And Antiquity. By Increase Mather, Teacher of a Church of Christ in Boston in New-England.] *pp.* (8), 27.
4° *Boston: Printed by John Foster in the Year* 1680.

Heaven's Alarm to the World Or a Sermon, Wherein is Showed, That Fearful Sights and Signs in Heaven, are the Presages of Great Calamities at hand. Preached at the Lecture of Boston in New England; Jan'y 20, 1680. The Latter Sign Discoursed of in a Sermon Preached at the Lecture of Boston, in New England, August 31, 1682. Wherein is Shewed, that the Voice of God in Signal Providences, especially when Repeated and Iterated, ought to be Hearkened unto. Second Impression. *pp. (8), 38, 32.*

        8° Boston: Printed for Samuel Sewall, 1682.

Practical Truths Tending to Promote the Power of Godliness : Wherein Several Important Duties, are Urged, and the Evil of divers common Sins, is Evinced : Delivered in Sundry Sermons. *pp. (14), 220.*

    Sm. 8° *Boston in New-England. Printed by Samuel Green upon Assignment of Samuel Sewall,* 1682.

    Thomas quotes a second edition with the same imprint.

A Sermon Wherein is shewed that the Church of God is sometimes a Subject of Great Persecution ; Preached on a Publick Fast at Boston in New-England : Occasioned by the Tidings of a great Persecution Raised against the Protestants in France. *pp. (6), 24.*

    4° *Boston, in New-England: Printed for Samuel Sewall, in the Year* 1682.

Κομητογραφια. Or a Discourse Concerning Comets ; Wherein the Nature of Blazing Stars is Enquired into : With an Historical Account of all the Comets which have appeared from the Beginning of the World unto this present Year, M.DC.LXXXIII. Expressing the Place in the Heavens, where they were seen, Their Motion, Forms, Duration ; and the Remarkable Events which have followed in the World, so far as they have been by Learned Men Observed. As also two Sermons, Occasioned by the late Blazing Stars. By Increase Mather, Teacher of a Church at Boston in New-England. *pp. (12), 143.*

    Sm. 8° *Boston in New-England. Printed by S[amuel] G[reen] for S[amuel] S[ewall], And sold by J. Brunning At the corner of the Prison Lane next the Town-House,* 1683.

    An Address "To the Reader," p. 4, is signed "John Sherman." The "two Sermons" are, "Heaven's Alarm. Second Impression, 1682," which has a separate title-page, and "The Latter Sign," which has continuous signatures with "Heaven's Alarm."

The Doctrine of Divine Providence opened and Applyed. Also Sundry Sermons on Several Other Subjects. *pp. (7), 148.*

        8° Boston: Printed by Richard Pierce, 1684.

A Sermon (Preached at the Lecture in Boston in New-England the 18th of the I. Moneth 1674. When two men were Executed, who had Murthered their Master). Wherein is Shewed That Excess in Wickedness doth bring Untimely Death. The Second Impression. By Increase Mather, Teacher of a Church of Christ. *pp. (2), 38.*

    Sm. 8°, *Printed by R. P[ierce], for J. Brunning in Boston,* 1685.

    For first Edition, see page 23, "The Wicked Man's Portion." 1675.

The Mystery of Christ opened and applyed. In several Sermons, Concerning the Person, Office, and Glory of Jesus Christ. By Increase Mather, Teacher of· a Church at Boston in N. England. *pp. (2) 6, 212, (1).*

    Sm. 8° *Boston: Printed at Boston in New England Anno* 1686.

The Greatest Sinners Exhorted and Encouraged To Come to Christ and that Now Without Delaying. Also, The Exceeding Danger of Men's Deferring their Repentance. Together with a Discourse about The Day of Judgement. And on Several other Subjects. *pp. (4), 146.*

    Sm. 8° *Boston: Joseph Browning,* 1686.

A Sermon Occasioned by the Execution of (James Morgan) a Man found Guilty of Murder: Preached at Boston, in New England, March 11th, $168\frac{6}{7}$ [sic]. (Together with the Confession, Last Expressions, and Solemn Warning of that Murderer; *Especially* to Young Men, to beware of *those* Sins which brought him to his *Miserable End.*) The Second Edition. *pp. (4)*, 124.
    8° *Boston: Printed by R[ichard] P[ierce]. Sold by J. Brunning. Anno*   1687.

    Pages 37–82 of the second edition, whose title varies somewhat from the first, contain " The Call of the Gospel," with a title-page, and " An Exhortation," with a title-page.

A Testimony Against several Prophane and Superstitious Customs, Now Practised by some in New-England, The Evil whereof is evinced from the Holy Scriptures, and from the Writings both of Ancient and Modern Divines. *pp. (8)*, 41.
    Sm. 8° *London: Printed in the Year* 1687.

    Thomas quotes an edition " *Boston. Reprinted from the London Edition.*" 1688.

A Brief Discourse Concerning the unlawfulness of the Common Prayer Worship, and Of Laying the Hand on, and Kissing the Booke in Swearing. By a Reverend and Learned Divine. The Second Impression. *pp. (2)*, 43.
    Sm. 8° *Reprinted at London in the Year* 1689.

The Present State of New England impartially considered in a Letter to the Clergy. *pp.* 44.   4° *London*, 1689.

The Revolution in New England Justified and the People there Vindicated from the Aspersions cast upon them by Mr. John Palmer, in his Pretended Answer to the Declaration, Published by the Inhabitants of Boston, and the Country adjacent, on the day when they secured their late Oppressors, who acted by an Illegal and Arbitrary Commission from the Late King James. *pp. (6)*, 48.
    4° *Printed for Joseph Brunning at Boston in New-England*, 1691.

    " To the Reader," is signed by " E. R." and " S. S." which it is said represent Edward Rawson and Samuel Sewall.

    There is another edition of this work in the Library with the same title, and, " To which is added, A Narrative of the Proceedings of Sir Edmond Androsse and his Accomplices, who also acted by an Illegal and Arbitrary Commission from the late King James, during his Government in New England." By several Gentlemen who were of his Council. 8°. pp. 59. Printed in the Year 1692. Boston: Reprinted and sold by Isaiah Thomas. . . . MDCCLXXXIII.

A Further Account of the Tryals of the New-England Witches. With the Observations Of a Person who was upon the Place several Days when the suspected Witches were first taken into Examination. To which is added Cases of Conscience Concerning Witchcrafts and Evil Spirits Personating men. Written at the Request of the Ministers of New-England. By Increase Mather, President of Harvard Colledge. Licensed and Entred according to Order. *pp.* 10, *(4)*, 40, *(4)*.
    4° *London: Printed for J. Dunton at the Raven in the Poultrey*,   1693.

    The last four pages contain a list of " Books now in the Press, and going to it. Printed for John Dunton, at the Raven in Poultry."

4

The Great Blessing, of Primitive Counsellours. Discoursed in a Sermon, Preached in the Audience of the Governour, Council, and Representatives, of the Province of the Massachusets-Bay, in New-England. May 31st, 1693. Being the Day for the Election of Counsellours, in that Province. *pp.* 23.
4° *Boston: Printed by Benjamin Harris,* 1693.

The Answer Of Several Ministers in and near Boston, To that Case of Conscience, Whether it is Lawful for a Man to Mary his Wives own Sister ? *pp.* 8, (1).
Sm. 8° *Boston in N. E., Printed and Sold by Bartholomew Green,* 1695.

The "Answer" is signed by Increase Mather, Charles Morton. James Allen, Samuel Willard. James Sherman. John Danforth, Cotton Mather, Nehemiah Walter; and is against such marriages. It is followed by an obituary notice of Mrs. Judith Hull, which may be a separate publication, and is probably by Cotton Mather.

Angelographia, or A Discourse Concerning the Nature and Power of the Holy Angels, and the Great Benefit which the True Fearers of God Receive by their Ministry : Delivered in several Sermons : To which is added, A Sermon concerning the Sin and Misery of the Fallen Angels : Also a Disquisition concerning Angelical-Apparitions. By Increase Mather, President of Harvard Colledge, in Cambridge, and Preacher of the Gospel at Boston in New-England. *pp.* (16), 132, 44. Sm. 8° *Boston in N. E., Printed by B. Green & J. Allen, for Samuel Phillips,* 1696.

David Serving His Generation. Or, A Sermon Shewing What is to be done in order to our so Serving our Generation, as that when we Dy, we shall Enter into a Blessed Rest. Occasioned by the Death, of the Reverend Mr. John Baily, who deceased at Boston in New-England, December 12th, 1697. *pp.* 39.
Sm. 8° *Boston, Printed by B. Green & J. Allen,* 1698.

Masukkenukeeg Matcheseaenvog Wequetoog kah Wuttoonnatoog Uppevaonont Christoh kah ne Yeuyeu Teanuk Wonk, ahche nunnukquodt missinninnuk ukquohquenaount wutaiuskoianntamooonganoo. Kah Keketookuonk papaume Wussittumwae kesukodtum. Kah papaume nawhutch onkatogch Wunnomwayeuongash Nashpe Increase Mather. Kukkootomwehteanenuh ut oomoeuwehkomonganit ut Bostonut, ut New England. Yeush kukkookootomwehteaongash qushkinnumunash en Indiane unnontoowaonganit nashpe S. D[anforth]. *pp.* 164.
Sm. 8° *Bostonut, Printuoop Nashpe Bartholomew Green kah John Allen,* 1698.

Five sermons by Increase Mather, translated into the Indian language by Rev. Samuel Danforth. " The first Indian book known to have been printed after the removal of the press to Boston."—J. H. TRUMBULL in *A. A. S. Proceedings,* No. 61.

The Order of the Gospel, Professed and Practised by the Churches of Christ in New-England, Justified, by the Scripture, and by the Writings of many Learned men, both Ancient and Modern Divines; In Answer to several Questions, relating to Church Discipline. *pp.* 143, (1).
12° *Boston, Printed by B. Green & J. Allen, for Benjamin Eliot,* 1700.

More commonly cited by its running title, " The Order of the Churches in N. England Vindicated."

The Blessed Hope, And the Glorious Appearing of the Great God our Saviour, Jesus Christ. Opened & Applied, In several Sermons. By Increase Mather, President of Harvard College in Cambridge And Preacher of the Gospel at Boston in N. E. *pp.* 142.
Sm. 8° *Boston, Printed by Timothy Green, for N. Boone,* 1701.

A Discourse Proving that the Christian Religion, Is the only True Religion: Wherein, The necessity of Divine Revelation is Evinced, in several Sermons. *pp.* (4), 96. *Boston, Timothy Green,* 1702.

The Excellency of a Publick Spirit Discoursed : In a Sermon, Preached in the Audience of the General Assembly of the Province of the Massachusetts Bay in New-England May 27, 1702. Being the day for Election of Counsellors in that Province. By Increase Mather. [Followed by:] The Righteous Man A Blessing: Or, Seasonable Truths Encouraging unto Faith and Prayer in this Day of Doubtful Expectation. In Two Sermons. [And] The Morning Star. *pp.* (12), 84.
12° *Boston, in New-England, Printed by B. Green & J. Allen, for Nicholas Boone,* 1702.

Some Remarks On a late Sermon, Preached at Boston in New-England, by George Keith, M. A. Shewing That his pretended Good Rules in Divinity, are not built on the foundation of the Apostles & Prophets. *pp.* (2), 36. 16° *Boston, Printed for Nicholas Boone,* 1702.

Practical Truth's, Tending to Promote Holliness in the Hearts & Lives of Christians, Delivered in Several Sermons. *pp.* 102, (4).
12° *Boston in N. E., Printed by Barth. Green for Benj. Eliot,* 1704.

The Voice of God, in Stormy Winds. Considered, in Two Sermons, Occasioned by the Dreadful and Unparallel'd Storm, in the European Nations. Novemb. 27th. 1703. [Followed by:] A Brief Discourse Concerning the Prayse Due to God, for His Mercy, in giving Snow like Wool. *pp.* 95.
12° *Boston in N. E., Printed by T. Green for Nicholas Buttolph,* 1704.

"In the first tract, the address 'To the Reader' contains a brief notice of the attack on Deerfield and the capture of Mr. Williams and his family. The discourse makes frequent allusions to recent events: the great snow of Dec. 1703, and the loss of a Boston ship, in the harbor (p. 8), the storm of April 7th and 8th, 1704, which wrecked the French privateer 'designing to do us hurt' (p. 23), the terrible 'windy tempest' at Cambridge, in 1682, (pp. 63-4), etc."—*Sabin.*

A Letter. About the Present State of Christianity, among the Christianized Indians of New-England. Written, To the Honourable, Sir William Ashurst, Governour of the Corporation, for Propagating the Gospel among the Indians, in New-England, and Parts Adjacent, in America. *pp.* 15.
Sm. 8° *Boston in N. E., Printed by Timothy Green,* 1705.
Signed "Increase Mather, Cotton Mather, Nehemiah Walter."

Meditations on the Glory of the Lord Jesus Christ: Delivered in several Sermons. By Increase Mather. *pp.* (2), viii, 165, (1).
16° *Boston in New-England, Printed by Bartholomew Green, for Benj. Eliot,* 1705.

"In the Epistle Dedicatory, to his Congregation, April 2, 1705, the author says: 'You are to look upon these as *the Last Words*, which I shall ever, *by the Press*, Speak and Dedicatate (*sic*) unto you.' Nevertheless, he lived to publish more than thirty works after this (besides prefaces. dedications, etc.) Some copies have the imprint, *Boston in New-England: Printed by Bartholomew Green for Nicholas Buttolph, at the Corner of Gutteridges Coffee-House.*"

A Discourse Concerning Earthquakes. Occasioned by the Earthquakes which were in New-England, in the Province of Massachusetts Bay, June 16, and in Conecticot-Colony, June 22, 1705. Also, Two Sermons, shewing, That Sin is the Greatest Evil; And, That to Redeem Time is the Greatest Wisdom. *pp.* 181.
12° *Boston, Printed by Timothy Green, for Benjamin Eliot,* 1706.

A Discourse Concerning the Maintenance Due to those That Preach the Gospel; In Which That Question Whether Titles are by the Divine LAW the Ministers Due, is Considered, and the Negative Proved. *pp.* 60 (1). 12° *Boston,* 1706.
Also, An Edition, "Reprinted at London. 1709." 8°, pp. (4), 32.

A Plea for the Ministers Of the Gospel, Offered to the Consideration of the People of New-England. By a Friend to the Churches. *pp.* 29.
Sm. 8° *Boston Printed by B. Green,* 1706.

Meditations on Death. Delivered in Several Sermons. Wherein is Shewed: I. That some True Believers on Christ are afraid of Death, but that they have no Just Cause to be so. II. That Good Men as well as others may be taken out of the World by a Sudden Death. III. That not Earth but Heaven is the Christians Home. *pp.* v, 171, (5).
8° *Boston in N. E. Printed by Timothy Green,* 1707.

A Dissertation, wherein The Strange Doctrine Lately Published in a Sermon, The Tendency of which, is, to Encourage Unsanctified Persons (while such), to Approach the Holy Table of the Lord, is Examined and Confuted. With an Appendix, Shewing what Scripture Ground there is to Hope, that Within a very few years there will be a Glorious Reformation of the Church throughout the World. *pp.* (12), 135.

The preface is historical. It is in answer to Solomon Stoddard, who replied in "An Appeal to the Learned."

A Dissertation Concerning the Future Conversion of The Jewish Nation. Answering the Objections of the Reverend and Learned Mr. Baxter, Dr. Lightfoot, and others. With an Enquiry into the First Resurrection. *pp.* (4), 35. (1).
4° *London: Printed by R. Tookey for Nath. Hiller,* MDCCIX.

A Discourse Concerning the Grace of Courage, Wherein the Nature, Beneficialness, and Necessity of that Vertue for all Christians, is described. Delivered in a Sermon Preached at Boston in New-England [at the Artillery Election]. June 5th, 1710. *pp.* (4), 44.
12° *Boston: Printed by B. Green, for Samuel Phillips,* 1710.

An Earnest Exhortation to the Children of New-England, To Exalt the God of their Fathers. Delivered in a Sermon. *pp.* (4), 39.
12° *Boston, in N. E.: Benj. Eliot,* 1711.

Meditations on the Glory of the Heavenly World. I. On the Happiness of the Souls of Believers, at the Instant of their Separation from their Bodies. II. On the Glory of the Bodies of God's Children, in the Resurrection World, when they shall be as the Angels of Heaven. III. On the Glory of both Soul and Body in the Heaven of Heavens, after the Day of Judgment, to all Eternity. *pp.* (2), v, (1), 276, (4).
Sm. 8° *Boston in N. E. Printed: Sold by Benj. Eliot,* 1711.

"These Sermons were Pluckt out of the Burning; when Seven Booksellers Shops in Boston were Consumed in those Flames, which on the Second of this Instant October, made a dismal Desolation in the midst of this Great Town."—*Preface, pp. ii, iii.*

Burnings Bewailed: In a Sermon, Occasioned by the Lamentable Fire Which was in Boston, Octob. 2, 1711. In which the Sins which Provoke the Lord to Kindle Fires, are Enquired into. The Second Edition. *pp. (4)*, 36.
Sm. 8° *Boston in N. E.: Printed and Sold by Timothy Green,* 1712.

Meditations On the Sanctification of the Lord's Day: And On the Judgements which attend the Profanation of it. To which is Added, Seasonable Meditations both for Winter and Summer. *pp. (2)*, x, 71, *(3)*, iv, 51.
12° *Boston: Printed by T. G., for S. Gerrish,* 1712.

The "Seasonable Meditations" have a separate title-page, and were printed by *John Allen.*

Soul-Saving Gospel Truths. Deliver'd in several Sermons: Wherein is shew'd. I. The Unreasonableness of those Excuses which Men make for their Delaying to come to the Lord Jesus Christ for Salvation. II. That for Men to Despair of the Forgiveness of their Sins because they have been Great, is a great Evil. III. That every Man in the World is going into Eternity. Second Edition. *pp.* iv, 135.
24° *Boston:* 1712.

Wo to Drunkards. Two Sermons Testifying against the Sin of Drunkenness: Wherein the Wofulness of that Evil, and the Misery of all that are addicted to it, is Discovered from the Word of God. By Increase Mather, D.D. The Second Edition. *pp. (4)*, 58, *(1)*.
Sm. 8° *Boston: Printed by Timothy Green,* 1712.

Now or Never Is The Time for Men to make Sure of their Eternal Salvation. Several Sermons, In which is Declared; I. That Now is the Day of Salvation. II. That it is Wisdom, for Men to Consider their Latter End. III. That Impenitent Sinners will be found Guilty of their Own Destruction. *pp. (2)*, 2, 113. 8° *Boston,* 1713.

A copy of this was also received from the Brinley library.

A Disquisition Concerning Ecclesiastical Councils. Proving, that not only Pastors, But Brethren delegated by the Churches, have equally a Right to a decisive Vote in such Assemblies. To which is added, Proposals concerning Consociation of Churches, Agreed upon by a Synod, which Convened at Boston, in New-England. With a Preface, containing a further Vindication of the Congregational Discipline. *pp. (2)*, xx, 47, *(1)*. 12° *Boston, Printed for N. Boone,* 1716.

Also a reprint. Boston, 1870. 8°, pp. 36.

Practical Truths, Plainly Delivered: Wherein is Showed, 1. That true Believers on Jesus Christ, shall as certainly enjoy Everlasting Life in Heaven, as if they were there already. 2. That there is a blessed marriage between Jesus Christ the Son of God, & the true Believer. 3. That Men are Infinitely concerned, not only to hear the Voice of Christ, but that they do it, To-Day. 4. The Work of the Ministry, described, in an Ordination Sermon. *pp.* (4), 138. 12° *Boston,* 1718.

"The Work of the Ministry" has an independent title page.

A Sermon Wherein is Shewed, 1. That the Ministers of the Gospel need, and ought to desire the Prayers of the Lord's People for them. 2. That the People of God ought to Pray for his Ministers. Preached at Roxbury, October 29, 1718. When Mr. Thomas Walter Was Ordained a Pastor in that Church, by his Grand-Father, Increase Mather, D. D. *pp. (2)*, ii, 35, *(1)*.
8° *Boston, Printed by S. Kneeland, for J. Edwards,* 1718.

Sermons wherein Those Eight Characters of the Blessed Commonly called the Beatitudes, Are Opened & Applied in Fifteen Discourses. To which is added, A Sermon concerning Assurance of the Love of Christ. *pp.* (2), iv, 298.
        8° *Boston, N. E., Printed by B. Green, for Daniel Henchman,* 1718.

Five Sermons on Several Subjects. 1. A Birth Day Sermon, Preached on the Day When the Author Attained to the Eightieth Year of his Age. 2. A Dying Testimony to the Sovereign Grace of God in the Salvation of His Elect, Containing Three Sermons. 3. Believers encouraged to Pray. *pp.* v. 148.   12° *Boston,* 1719.

Awakening Soul-Saving Truths Plainly Delivered In Several Sermons in which is shewed, 1. That Many are Called, who are not effectually Called. 2. That Men may be of the Visible Church, and yet not be of the Lords Church. 3. That the Chosen of God are comparatively Few. *pp.* (2), II, 100, (1).
        12° *Boston, Printed by S. Kneeland for B. Gray and J. Edwards,*
                                                                        1720.

A Seasonable Testimony To Good Order in the Churches Of the Faithful. Particularly Declaring the Usefulness & Necessity of Councils in Order to Preserving Peace and Truth in the Churches. By Increase Mather, D.D. With the Concurrence of Other Ministers of the Gospel in Boston. *pp.* (4), 20.
        Sm. 8° *Boston, N. E., Printed by B. Green for D. Henchman,* 1720.

Advice to the Children of Godly Ancestors. Given July 9, 1721. By Increase Mather. And taken in Short-Hand, by one of the Hearers. *pp.* 16.   12° *Boston, Printed by S. Kneeland,* 1721.

        This " Advice," given in his eighty-third year, " without using any notes," is in " A Course of Sermons," the preface to which, is also by Increase Mather.

Some Important Truths About Conversion, Delivered in Sundry Sermons, By Increase Mather. With a Preface by Dr. Owen. The Second Edition. *pp.* (2), xxii, 260, (1).
        12° *London, Printed,* 1674.   *Boston, in N. E., Re-Printed by John Allen, for John Edwards,*   1721.

A Call to the Tempted. A Sermon on the horrid Crime of Self Murder, Preached on a Remarkable Occasion, by the Memorable Dr. Increase Mather. And now Published form his Notes, for a Charitable Stop to Suicides. *pp.* 4, 11, 17.   Sm. 8° *Boston,* 1723-4.

Ichabod. Or, A Discourse, Shewing what Causes there is to Fear that the Glory Of the Lord, is Departing from New England. Delivered in Two Sermons. Second edition. *pp.* 88.
                        12° *Boston, Printed for N. Boone,* 1729.
        The first Edition was received from the Brinley Library.

Remarkable Providences Illustrative of the Earlier Days of American Colonization. By Increase Mather. With an Introductory Preface, by George Offer. *pp.* XIX., (18), 262. Portrait.
                        8° *London: John Russell Smith,* 1856.

The History of King Philip's War. By the Rev. Increase Mather, D.D. Also, a History of the Same War, by the Rev. Cotton Mather, D.D. To which is added An Introduction and Notes, By Samuel G. Drake. *pp.* 281. 2 Portraits, Pedigree of the Mather family, folded sheet.
        4° *Boston: Printed for the Editor, By J. Munsell,* 1862.

"This is a new edition of 'A Brief History,' (Page 23.) Two hundred and sixty-one copies printed, of which eleven are on large paper. The editor has marred the completeness of this edition by reproducing the abridged text of Cotton Mather's 'Troubles ... had with the Indian Salvages,' from Book VII. of his 'Magnalia,' blended with the material of the other work. Pages 227-264 consist of narratives, etc., now first printed."

Early History of New England; being a Relation of Hostile Passages between the Indians and European Voyagers and First Settlers: and a full Narrative of Hostilities, to the Close of the War with the Pequots, in the year 1637; Also a Detailed account of the Origin of the War with King Philip. By Increase Mather. With an Introduction and Notes, By Samuel G. Drake. *pp.* 319.

4° *Boston : Printed for the Editor,* 1864.

COTTON MATHER.

Military Duties, Recommended to an Artillery Company; at their Election of Officers, in Charlestown, 13. d. 7. m. 1686. By Cotton Mather, Pastor of a Church in Boston. *pp. (8), 78, (2).*

Sm. 8° *Boston in New England. Printed by Richard Pierce: And are to be sold by Joseph Brunning, at his Shop at the Corner of Prison Lane near the Exchange,* · 1687.

Memorable Providences, Relating to Witchcrafts And Possessions. A Faithful Account of many Wonderful and Surprising Things, that have befallen several Bewitched and Possessed Persons in New-England. Particularly, A Narrative of the Marvellous Trouble and Releef [*sic*], Experienced by a Pious Family in Boston, very lately and sadly molested with Evil Spirits. Whereunto is added, A Discourse delivered unto a Congregation in Boston, on the Occasion of that Illustrious Providence. As also A Discourse delivered unto the same Congregation: on the occasion of an horrible Self-Murder Committed in the Town. With an Appendix, in vindication of a Chapter in a late Book of Remarkable Providences, from the Calumnies of a Quaker at Pensilvania. Written By Cotton Mather, Minister of the Gospel. And Recommended by the Ministers of Boston and Charleston. *pp. (10), 75, 21, 40, (2), 14.*

Sm. 8° *Printed at Boston in N. England by R. P.* 1680. *Sold by Joseph Brunning, at his Shop at the Corner of the Prison-Lane next to the Exchange,* 1689.

The first of the two appended discourses is "On the Power and Malice of the Devils;" the second is "A Discourse on Witchcraft." The Appendix (lacking in Society's copy) (pp. 14) contains a reply to George Keith's "Churches in New-England brought to the Test," etc.

Souldiers Counselled and Comforted. A Discourse Delivered unto some part of the Forces Engaged in the Just War of New-England Against the Northern and Eastern Indians. Sept. 1, 1689. By Cotton Mather, Minister of the Gospel in Boston. *pp. (10),* 38. Sm. 8° *Boston, N. E. Printed by Samuel Green,* 1689.

A Companion for Communicants. Discourses Upon The Nature, the Design, and the Subject of the Lords Supper; With Devout Methods of Preparing for and Approaching to that Blessed Ordinance. *pp. (8), 167, (1).*

Sm. 8° *Printed at Boston by Samuel Green for Benjamin Harris,* 1690.

The Principles of the Protestant Religion Maintained, And Churches o f New-England, in the Profession and Exercise thereof Defended, Against all the Calumnies of one George Keith, a Quaker, in a book lately Published at Pensilvania, to undermine them both. By the Ministers of the Gospel in Boston. *pp.* (10), 156.

Sm. 8° *Boston, in New-England, Printed by Richard Pierce,* MDCXC.

The preface is signed "James Allen, Joshuah Moodey, Samuel Willard, Cotton Mather."

The Serviceable Man. A Discourse Made unto the General Court of the Massachusetts Colony, New England, At the Anniversary Election 28d. 3m, 1690. *pp.* (4), 64.

Sm. 8° *Boston, Printed by Samuel Green for Joseph Brunning,* 1690.

The Way to Prosperity. A Sermon Preached to the Honourable Convention Of the Governour, Council, and Representatives of the Massachuset-Colony in New-England; on May 23, 1689. By Cotton Mather. *pp.* (7), 26 [*i. e.* 36], 5, (7).

Sm. 8° *Boston, Printed by Joseph Brunning, Obadiah Gill and James Woode.* MDCXC.

Fair Weather. Or Considerations to Dispel the Clouds, & Allay the Storms of Discontent, in a Discourse which with an Entertaining Variety, both of Argument and History, layes open. the Nature and Evil of that Pernicious Vice, and offers divers Antidotes against it. Whereto there is prefixed a Catalogue of Sins against all the Commandments. *pp.* (2), 93.

12° *Boston: Printed by B. Green and John Allen, for Benjamin Harris,* 1691.

Appended (pp. 83-92) is "A Narrative of a Very Tragical Accident, which happened while the foregoing Treatise was in the Press,"—the assault on York, by the Eastern Indians: with an Epitaph on Rev. Shubael Dummer who was killed.

The Life and Death Of The Renown'd Mr. John Eliot, Who was the First Preacher of the Gospel to the Indians in America. With an Account of the Wonderful Success which the Gospel has had amongst the Heathen in that part of the World: And of the many strange Customes of the Pagan Indians, In New England. The Second Edition carefully corrected. *pp.* (6), 138.

Sm. 8° *London, Printed for John Dunton,* M DC XCI.

Autograph of *Samuel Mather.*

Little Flocks Guarded against Grievous Wolves. An Address Unto those Parts of New-England which are most Exposed unto Assaults, from the Modern Teachers of the misled Quakers. (In a letter, Which impartially Discovers the manifold Halresies and Blasphemies, and the Strong Delusions of even the most Refined Quakerism; And thereupon Demonstrates the Truth of those Principles and Assertions, which are most opposite thereunto.) With just Reflections upon the extreom Ignorance and Wickedness, of George Keith, Who is the Seducer that now most Ravines upon the Churches in this Wilderness. *pp.* (2), 110.

8° *Boston: Printed by Benjamin Harris & John Allen,* 1691.

The Triumphs of the Reformed Religion, in America. The Life of the Renowned John Eliot; A Person justly Famous in the Church of God, Not only as an Eminent Christian, and an Excellent Minister, among the English, But also, As a Memorable Evangelist among the Indians, of New-England; With some Account concerning the late and Strange Success of the Gospel, in those parts of the World, which for many Ages have lain Buried in Pagan Ignorance. Written by Cotton Mather. *pp. (8), 182.*

    8° Boston: Printed by Benjamin Harris, and John Allen, for Joseph Brunning, 1691.

Blessed Unions. An Union With the Son of God, by Faith, And, an Union In the Church of God by Love, Importunately Pressed; in a Discourse Which makes Divers Offers, for those Unions; Together with A Copy of those Articles, whereupon a most Happy Union, has been lately made between those two Eminent Parties in England, which have now Changed the names of Presbyterians and Congregationals for that of United Brethren. *pp. (10), 86, 12.*

    24° Boston: Printed by B. Green, & J. Allen, 1692.

    The "Articles" were also printed in the "Magnalia." v. 58-61, *for Samuel Phillips.*

A Midnight Cry. An Essay for our Awakening out of a Sinful Sleep. A Discourse given on a Day of Prayer, kept by the North-Church in Boston. *pp. 72.*

    12° Boston: Printed by John Allen, for Sam. Phillips, 1692.

    "I have ordered a *Small Impression.* So that perhaps I may say of this Book, as the Philosopher did of his, '*Tis Published, but Scarce made Publick.*"—*Preface.*

Unum Necessarium. Awakenings for the Unregenerate; or the Nature and Necessity of Regeneration. Handled in a Discourse designed for the service of any that may be thereby assisted in the Grand Concern of Conversion unto God; but especially the Rising Generation. With an Addition of some other Sermons relating to that Important Subject. *pp. vi., 154.*

    8° Boston, Printed by B. H. for Duncan Campbell, 1693.

Winter Meditations, Directions How to employ the Liesure [sic] of the Winter For the Glory of God. Accompanied with Reflections, as well Historical, as Theological, not only upon the Circumstances of the Winter, But also, upon the Notable Works of God, Both in, Creation, and Providence: Especially those, which more immediately Concern every Particular Man, in the whole course of his Life: And upon the Religious works, wherewith every Man should acknowledge God, in and from the Accidents of the Winter. With a Preface of the Reverend, Mr. John Higginson. *pp. (16), 82.*

    8° Boston, Printed by Benj. Harris, · 1693.

Early Religion, Urged in a Sermon, Upon The Duties Wherein, And the Reasons Wherefore, Young People, Should Become Religious, Whereto are Added, The Extracts of several Papers, Written by several Persons, who here Dying in their Youth, left behind them those Admonitions for the Young Survivers, with Brief Memoirs relating to the Exemplary Lives of some such, that have gone from hence to their Everlasting Rest. *pp. (2), 117, (1).*

    8° Boston, Printed by B. H., for Michael Perry, 1694.

Ornaments for the Daughters of Zion. Or The Character and Happiness of a Vertuous [sic] Woman: A Discourse. *pp. (12), 144.*

    12° Cambridge, Printed by S. G. & B. G., for Samuel Phillips, 1691, *London, Printed for Thos. Parkhurst,* 1694.

    Thomas in his " History of Printing " mentions an edition of 1682.

5

The Short History of New England. A Recapitulation of Wonderfull Passages Which have Occurr'd, First in the Protections, and then in the Afflictions of New England. With a Representation of Certain Matters calling for the Singular Attention of that Country. Made at Boston Lecture, in the Audience of the Great and General Assembly of the Province of the Massachusetts Bay. June 7, 1694. *pp.* 67.
12° *Boston, Printed by B. Green for S. Phillips,* 1694.

Brontologia Sacra: the Voice of the Glorious God in the Thunder: Explained and Applied In a Sermon uttered by a Minister of the Gospel in a Lecture unto an Assembly of Christians abroad, at the very same time when the Thunder was by the Permission and Providence of God falling upon his own House at home. Whereto are added some Reflections formed on the Lords Day following by the Voices of Thunders, upon the great things which the great God is now a doing in the World. A Discourse useful for all Men at all times, but especially intended for an Entertainment in the Hours of Thunder. *pp.* (4), 38. 16° *London, Printed by John Ashwood,* 1695.

Johannes in Eremo. Memoirs, Relating to the Lives, of the Ever-Memorable, Mr. John Cotton, Who Dyed, 23, d. 10, m. 1652. Mr. John Norton, Who Dyed, 5. d. 2. m. 663. Mr. John Wilson, Who Dyed, 7. d. 6. m. 1667. Mr. John Davenport, Who Dyed, 15. d. 1. m. 1670. Reverend and Renowned Ministers of the Gospel. All, in the more Immediate Service of One Church, in Boston; and Mr. Thomas Hooker, Who Dyed, 7. d. 5. m. 1647, Pastor of the Church at Hartford, New England. Written by Cotton Mather. *pp.* 32, 80, 39, 46, 30, 45, (2). Sm. 8° *Boston, Michael Perry,* 1695.

"To the Reader," 10 pp., by Increase Mather. After the Introduction, is the Advertisement of the author's projected "Church History of New England" (the "Magnalia"), with "A Schæme of the Whole Work." (pp. 28–32).

Piscator Evangelicus. Or, The Life of Mr. Thomas Hooker, The Renowned, Pastor of Hartford Church, and Pillar of Connecticut Colony, in New England essay'd by Cotton Mather. *pp.* 45, (2).
8° *Boston, Printed in the year* 1695.

The last two pages have "A Catalogue of some other Books, all by this Author," comprising thirty-four titles.

Memoria Wilsoniana. Or, Some Dues Unto The Memory of the Truly Reverend & Renowned Mr. John Wilson, The First Pastor of Boston: Who Expired August 7. 1667. Aged 79. Paid by Cotton Mather. *pp.* (2), 46.
Sm. 8° *Printed for and Sold by Michael Perry, in Boston, in N. E.* 1695.
Reprinted in "Johannes in Eremo."

The Christian Thank-Offering. A Brief Discourse Made on a Solemn Thanksgiving, kept in a Private Meeting of Christians, on the Occasion of some Deliverance. *pp.* 32.
8° *Boston, Printed by B. Green & J. Allen, for Michael Perry,* 1696.

A versified paraphrase of the 103d Psalm, by Mather, is prefixed.

Things for a Distress'd People to think upon. Offered in the Sermon to the General Assembly of the Province of the Massachusetts-Bay, at the Anniversary Election, May 27, 1696. By Cotton Mather. *pp.* (2), 84.
Sm. 8° *Boston, Printed by B. Green & J. Allen, for Duncan Campbel.* 1696.

Ecclesiastes. The Life of the Reverend & Excellent, Jonathan Mitchel; A Pastor of the Church, and A Glory of the Colledge, in Cambridge, New-England. Written by Cotton Mather. *pp.* 111, (32).
Sm. 8° *Massachuset, Printed by B. Green and J. Allen,* 1697.

Dedicatory Epistle by Increase Mather. At the end of the sermon are two elegies, in verse, one by Cotton Mather, the other, with an " Epitaphium," signed " F. D." [Francis Drake].

Eleutheria : or, An Idea of the Reformation In England : and A History of Non-Conformity in and since that Reformation. With Predictions of a more glorious Reformation and Revolution at hand. Written in the year 1696. Mostly compiled and maintain'd from unexceptionable Writings of Conformable Divines in the Church of England. To which is added, The Conformists Reasons for joining with the Non-conformists in Divine Worship. By another Hand. *pp.* 4, 185.
8° *London, Printed for J. R. and sold by Sam. Phillips, Bookseller at Boston, in New-England,* 1698.

With autograph of Samuel Mather.

La Fe del Christiano : En Veyntequatro Articulos de la Institucion de Christo. Embiada A Los Espanoles, Por C. Mathero, Sieno del Senor Jesu Christo. *pp.* 16. Sm. 8° *Boston,* 1699.

A Family Well-Ordered. Or An Essay To Render Parents and Children Happy In one another. Handling two very Important Cases. I. What are the Duties to be done by Pious Parents, for the promoting of Piety in their Children. II. What are the Duties that must be paid by Children to their Parents, that they may obtain the Blessings of the Dutiful. *pp.* 79, 5.
12° *Boston, Printed by B. Green and J. Allen for Michael Perry,* 1699.

At the end is " An Address *Ad Fratres in Eremo*," of five pages, separately paged.

Pillars of Salt. An History of some Criminals executed in this Land, For Capital Crimes. With some of their Dying Speeches ; Collected and Published, For the Warning of such as Lived in Destructive Courses of Ungodliness. Whereto is added, for the better improvement of this History, a Brief Discourse about the Dreadful Justice of God, in Punishing of Sin, with Sin. *pp.* 111.
Sm. 8° *Boston, in New England. Printed by B. Green and J. Allen, for Samuel Phillips,* 1699.

A Pillar of Gratitude. Or, A brief Recapitulation, of the Matchless Favours, with which the God of Heaven hath obliged the Hearty Praises of His New-English Israel. A Sermon delivered in the Audience of His Excellency, the Earl of Bellomont, Captain General, and Governor in Chief, and of the Council & Representatives, of the General Assembly of the Province of the Massachusetts-Bay, Convened at Boston, in New-England. On May 29, 1700, the Day, for Election of Counsellors, in that Province. Whereto there is Appendiced, an Extract of Some Accounts, concerning the Wonderful Success of the Glorious Gospel, in the East Indies. *pp.* 48.
12° *Boston, by B. Green & J. Allen,* 1700.

Things that Young People should Think upon. Or, The Death or Young People Improved, In some Lively Admonitions to the Living. With Consolations, to the Bereaved Parents of such Young People, as are by an Early, (and perhaps a Sudden) Death, taken from them. *pp.* 16 *and over.*
Sm. 8° *Boston in N. E. Printed by B. Green & J. Allen,* 1700.

A Warning to the Flocks against Wolves in Sheeps-Cloathing. Or, A Faithful Advice from several Ministers of the Gospel, in and near Boston, unto the Churches of New-England, relating to the Dangers that may arise from Impostors, pretending to be Ministers. With a Brief History of some Impostors. *pp.* 79, (1).

16° *Boston, Printed for the Booksellers,* 1700.

"A Letter Containing a Remarkable History of an Impostor" [Samuel May], dated 25 d. 10 m. 1699, signed by C. Mather, pp. 29-52; A Postscript, "Something to be Known by all the Churches," etc.

American Tears upon the Ruins of the Greek Churches. A Compendious, but Entertaining History of the Darkness come upon the Greek Churches, in Europe and Asia. Composed by an American. With An Appendix containing a Relation of the Conversion of a Jew, Named Shalome Ben Shalomoh. *pp.* 80.

16° *Boston in N. E. Printed by B. Green & J. Allen, for, and sold by Samuel Sewall Junior,* 1701.

The appendix has (p. 56) a separate title and imprint, with a preface (3 pp.) signed, "Cotton Mather."

A Companion for the Afflicted. The Duties and the Comforts of Good Men, under their Afflictions. In Two Brief and Plain Discourses. Accommodated unto the Condition That All at Some Times, and Some at All Times, do Encounter withal. *pp.* 56.

18° *Boston, in N. E. Printed by T. Green, for, and sold by Samuel Sewall Junior,* 1701.

Death made Easic & Happy. Two Discourses on the Prudent Apprehensions of Death. With Serious Thoughts in Dying Times: or, A Discourse upon Death. *pp.* (2), 106.

24° *London, Printed for Tho. Parkhurst,* 1701.

A Letter to Ungospellized Plantations, Briefly Representing the Excellency and Necessity of a People's Enjoying the Gospel of the Lord Jesus Christ among them, *pp.* 16.

8° *Boston, Printed by B. Green & J. Allen,* 1702.

Magnalia Christi Americana: or, the Ecclesiastical History of New-England, from Its First Planting in the Year 1620, unto the Year of our Lord, 1698. In Seven Books. To which is subjoined An Appendix of Remarkable Occurrences which New-England had in the Wars with the Indian Salvages, from the Year 1688, to the Year 1698. *pp.* (30), 38; (2), 75; (2), 238; (2), 125;—222; 100, (2), 88; 118; Errata (2). Folio, *London, Printed for Thomas Parkhurst,* MDCCII.

Also First American Edition from the London Edition of 1702. 2 Vols. 8° pp. 573; 595. Hartford, 1820. Published by Silas Andrus.

Another edition, also in two volumes, has in Vol. I. the imprint, Silas Andrus & Son, Hartford, 1855, but in Vol. II. the date is 1853. Both volumes are entered according to Act of Congress, 1852. Vol. 1. has a Memoir of Cotton Mather, by Samuel G. Drake,

Necessary Admonitions. Containing Just Thoughts upon some Sins, Too Little Thought of, or, A Brief Discourse Concerning Sins of Omissions. Made 11 d. 4 m. 1702. *pp.* (2), 34.

12° *Boston in N. E. Printed by B. Green & J. Allen for Samuel Phillips,* 1702.

The Pourtraiture of a Good Man, Drawn With the Pencils of the Sanctuary, in such Colours as the Oracles of the Sacred Scriptures have given him. At a Lecture, in the Audience of the General Assembly, at Boston, June 25, 1702. *pp.* 34.
Sm. 8° *Boston, Printed for, and sold by Benjamin Eliot,* 1702.

A Seasonable Testimony to the Glorious Doctrines of Grace, At this Day many ways undermined in the World. Considered. by a General Convention of Ministers, Meeting at Boston, May 28, 1702. And Voted by them, to he Published, for the Establishment of the Churches in the present Truth. *pp.* 15. Sm. 8° *Boston,* 1702.

The Day which the Lord hath made. A Discourse Concerning the Institution and Observation of the Lords-Day. Delivered in a Lecture, at Boston, 4 d. 1 m. 1703. *pp.* (2), 46.
Sm. 8° *Boston, N. E. Printed by B. Green, and J. Allen,* 1703.

A Family Sacrifice. A Brief Essay To Direct and Excite Family Religion; and Produce the Sacrifices of Righteousness in our Families. *pp.* (2) 40.
Sm. 8° *Boston, Printed by B. Green & J. Allen. Sold by B. Eliot,* 1703.

Meat out of the Eater. Or, Funeral-Discourses, Occasioned By the Death of several Relatives. Work accommodated unto the Service of all that are in any affliction; but very particularly such as are afflicted with the loss of their Consorts or Children. *pp.* (6), 222.
24° *Boston, Benjamin Eliot,* 1703.

The Retired Christian, Or, The Duty of Secret Prayer, Publickly inculcated; In a Sermon, at Boston Lecture, April 18, 1703. *pp.* 46.
12° *Boston, Printed by B. Green & J. Allen for S. Phillips,* 1703.

The Wonderful Works of God Commemorated. Praises Bespoke for the God of Heaven, In a Thanksgiving Sermon; Delivered on Decemb. 19, 1689. Containing Just Reflections upon the Excellent Things done by the Great God, more Generally in Creation and Redemption, and in the Government of the World; But more Particularly in the Remarkable Revolutions of Providence which are every where the Matter of present Observation. With a Postscript giving an Account of some very stupendous Accidents, which have lately happened in France. By Cotton Mather. To which is Added a Sermon Preached unto the Convention of the Massachusetts Colony in New England. With a short Narrative of several Prodigies, which New-England hath of late had the Alarms of Heaven in. *pp.* (8), 62, 7, 26 [36]. 5, 7.
Sm. 8° *Printed at Boston by S. Green and Sold by Joseph Browning at the corner of the Prison Lane and Benj. Harris at the London Coffee-House,* 1690. Second Edition. *Boston,* 1703.

The Armour of Christianity. A Treatise, Detecting first, the Plots of the Devil against our Happiness. Declaring then, the Wiles by which those Plots are managed. And Propounding, lastly, the Thoughts by which those Wiles may be Defeated. *pp.* (2), 234.
12° *Boston, in N. E. Printed by Timothy Green, for Benjamin Eliot,* 1704.

Baptistes: A Conference About the Subject and Manner of Baptism, Between C. M. and D. R. *pp.* (3), 32. 8° *Boston,* 1704.

A Faithful Monitor. Offering. An Abstract of the Lawes in the Province of the Massachusett-Bay. New-England, Against those Disorders, the

Suppression whereof is desired and pursued by them that wish well to the worthy Designs of Reformation. With some Directions and Encouragements, to dispense due Rebukes, & Censures unto all Censurable Actions. *pp.* 56.

Sm. 8° *Boston: Printed ... by Timothy Green,* 1704.

A Weaned Christian, Or, Some Good Things, By which a Serious Christian May be Made Easy When Great Things are Deny'd unto him. In a Brief Essay, to render the Language of Heaven in Multiplied Judgments upon the Earth, Articulate. *pp.* 42.

12° *Boston, Printed and sold by Timothy Green,* 1704.

A Faithful Man, Described and Rewarded. Some Observable & Serviceable Passages in the Life and Death of Mr. Michael Wigglesworth. Late Pastor of Maldon; Who Rested from his Labours, on the Lords-Day, June 10th. 1705. In the Seventy Fourth year of his Age. And Memorials of Piety, Left behind him among his Written Experiences. With a Funeral Sermon Preached (for him) at Maldon; June 24. By Cotton Mather. *pp.* (6), 48. 12° *Boston, Printed by B. Green,* 1705.

"The Dedication," pp. 4. is signed "Increase Mather." The "Written Experiences" fill pp. 27-48. On page 48 is a punning epitaph on Wigglesworth, in verse.

Lex Mercatoria. Or, The Just Rules of Commerce Declared. And Offences against the Rules of Justice in the Dealing of Men with one another Detected. With a Testimony Publickly given against all Dishonest Gain, in the Audience of the General Assembly of the Province of the Massachusetts-Bay, New England, Nov. 9, 1704. *pp.* 40.

Sm. 8° *Boston, Printed by Timothy Green,* 1705.

Free-Grace, Maintained & Improved. Or, The General Offer of the Gospel, Managed with Considerations of the Great Things done by Special Grace, in the Election and Redemption and Vocation Of those who Embrace that Offer, and The Illustrious Doctrines of Divine Predestination and Humane Impotency, Rescued from the Abuses. which they too frequently meet withal; And rendered (as they are) highly Useful to the Designs of Practical Piety. In Two brief Discourses; Published at the Desire of Some, who have been greatly Apprehensive of Growing Occasions for such Treatises. *pp.* (2), 70.

Sm. 8° *Boston, Printed by B. Green,* 1706.

The Best Ornaments of Youth. A Short Essay on the Good Things, which are found in Some, and should be found in All, Young People, and which Wherever they are found, Heaven will take a Favourable Notice of them. A Sermon. *pp.* 36.

12° *Boston, in N. E., Timothy Green,* 1707.

Frontiers Well-Defended. An Essay to Direct the Frontiers of a Countrey Exposed unto the Incursions of a Barbarous Enemy. How to behave themselves in their Uneasy Station? Containing Admonitions of Piety, Propos'd by the Compassion of some Friends unto their Welfare, to be Lodg'd in the Families of our Frontier Plantations. *pp.* 52. Sm. 8° *Boston, in N. E., Printed by T. Green,* 1707.

Followed by "The Fall of Babylon." pp. (2), 20.

The Spirit of Life entering into the Spiritually Dead. An Essay, to bring a Dead Soul into the Way, wherein the Quickening Spirit of God & of Grace, is to Hoped and Waited for; And to Prophesy over the Dry Bones in the Valley of Death, such Words of the Lord, as use to be the Vehicles of Life unto them. *pp.* 40.

Sm. 8° *Boston, in N. E., Printed and sold by Timothy Green,* 1707.

Corderius Americanus. An Essay upon The Good Education of Children. And what may Hopefully be Attempted, for the Hope of the Flock, in a Funeral Sermon upon Mr. Ezekiel Cheever. The Ancient and Honorable Master of the Free-School in Boston, who left off, but when Mortality took him off, in August, 1708, the ninety-fourth year of his age, With an Elegy and an Epitaph upon him. By one that was once a Scholar to him. *pp. (6), 34.*

$8°$ *Boston, Printed by John Allen, for Nicholas Boone,* 1708.

Also an edition printed at Boston, 1828. " To which is added A selection from the Poems of Cheever's Manuscript."

A Good Evening for the Best of Dayes. An Essay, To Manage an Action of Trespass, against Those who Mispend the Lords-Day Evening, In such Things as have a Tendency to Defeat the Good of the Day. A Sermon in the Audience of the General Assembly, at Boston, 4 d. 9 m. 1708. *pp. (6), 26.*

$8°$ *Boston, Printed by B. Green,* 1708.

Family-Religion urged. Or, Some Serious Considerations, offer'd to the Reason and Conscience of Every Prayerless Householder, with Plain Directions how the Gift of Prayer may be taught Persons of the Meanest Capacity To which is added, a select number of choice Hymn. *pp. 24.*

$12°$ *Boston,* 1709.

The Temple Opening. A Particular Church Considered as a Temple of the Lord. In a Sermon Preached on a Day, when such a Church was Gathered, and a Pastor to it Ordained. *pp. (2), 34.*

$24°$ *Boston, Printed by B. Green, for S. Phillips,* 1709.

Bonifacius. An Essay Upon the Good, that is to be Devised and Designed, by those Who Desire to Answer the Great End of Life, and to Do Good While they Live. A Book Offered, First, in General, unto all Christians, Then Unto Magistrates, Ministers, Physicians, Lawyers, Schoolmasters, etc. *pp. (2), 206.*

$16°$ *Boston, in New England, Printed by B. Green, for Samuel Gerrish,* 1710.

Christianity Demonstrated. An Essay to Consider the Sanctifying Work of Grace On the Minds of the Faithful, as a Noble Demonstration to the Truth of our Holy Religion. With an Exhortation unto All but especially unto Young Persons, to seek after that Work of God. *pp.* 60.

$16°$ *Printed at Boston, in N. E. Sold by Timothy Green,* 1710.

Man Eating the Food of Angels. The Gospel of the Manna, To be Gathered in the Morning. With diverse famous & wondrous Examples of Early Piety, Especially, the Surprising History, of Christlieb Leberecht Von Extor, Late Son to the Physician of the King of Prussia. Delivered, part of it, in Boston-Lecture; part of it on another Occasion. *pp. (2), 85, (1).*

$12°$ *Boston, Printed for T. Green,* 1710.

Nehemiah. A Brief Essay on Divine Consolations, How Great they are; And How Great the Regards to be Paid unto them. With An Application thereof to Some frequent Cases, Especially The Death of Relatives. Offered, at the Lecture in Boston, 30 d. 9 m. 1710. By Cotton Mather, D. D. *pp. (4), 24.*

$4°$ *Boston, in New-England, Printed by Bartholomew Green,* 1710.

Theopolis Americana. An Essay on the Golden Street of the Holy City; publishing a Testimony against the Corruptions of the Market-

Place. With Some Good Hopes of Better Things to be yet seen in the American World. In a Sermon to The General Assembly of the Massachusett-Province in New England. 3 d. 9 m., 1709. *pp. (4), 51, (2).*

12° *Boston: Printed by B. Green,* 1710.

Winthropi Justa. A Sermon At the Funeral of the Hou'ble John Winthrop, Esq. Late Governour of the Colony of Connecticut in New-England. Who Died at Boston, Nov. 27, 1707, in his 69th Year. *pp. 40.*

8° *Printed at Boston in New-England, and Reprinted at London, by B. Harris,* 1710.

Manly Christianity. A Brief Essay on the Signs of Good Growth and Strength In the most Lovely Christianity. *pp. 34.*

Sm. 8° *London: For Ralph Smith,* 1711.

Perswasions [*sic*] from the Terror of the Lord. A Sermon concerning, The Day of Judgement; Preached on a Solemn Occasion, 15.d. 2.m. 1711. *pp. (2), 38.*

8° *Boston in New-England: Printed by Timothy Green,* 1711.

The Right Way to Shake off a Viper. An Essay on a Case Too Commonly calling for Consideration; What Shall Good Men do, when they are Evil Spoken of? *pp. (xi.), 35.*

8° *London: Printed and are to be sold by Sarah Popping at the Raven in Pater-Noster Row,* 1711.

Grace Defended. A Censure on Ungodliness, By which the Grace of God is too Commonly Abused. A Sermon Preached on the Twenty-fifth Day of December, 1712. Containing Some Seasonable Admonitions of Piety. And Concluded, with a brief Dissertation on the Penitent Thief on the Cross. By Cotton Mather, DD. *pp. (2), 35, (1).*

8° *Boston: Printed by B. Green, for Samuel Gerrish,* 1712.

("One of the earliest—perhaps the first—*Christmas Sermon* preached from a puritan pulpit in New England."—J. H. TRUMBULL.)

The Old Paths Restored. In a Brief Demonstration that the Doctrines of Grace hitherto Preserved in the Churches of the Non-Conformists, are not only Asserted in the Sacred Scriptures, but also in the Articles and Homilies of the Church of England; And That the General Departure from those Doctrines, Especially in those who have Subscribed them, is a Most Unaccountable Apostacy. *pp. 12, 24.*

Sm. 8° *Boston: Printed and Sold by T. Green, in Middle Street, 1711, And Reprinted at London,* 1712. With a Preface by Will. Whiston, A. M. *To be sold by A. Baldwin,* 1712.

A Soul Well-Anchored. A Little Manual for Self-Examination; To assist a Christian In Examining his Hopes of a Future Blessedness. *pp. 24.* 12° *Boston: Printed by B. Green,* 1712.

Thoughts for the Day of Rain. In Two Essay's I. The Gospel of the Rainbow. In the Meditations of Piety, on the Appearance of the Bright Clouds, with the Bow of God upon them. II. The Saviour with His Rainbow. And the Covenant which God will Remember to His People in the Cloudy Times that are passing over them. By Cotton Mather, D.D. *pp. (2), vi. 64.*

8° *Boston in N. E. Printed by B. Green: Sold by Samuel Gerrish,* 1712.

A True Survey & Report of the Road. A Brief Essay to Rectify the Mistakes of Men, about the Way taken by them. The Whole Way of

Transgression, and Particularly, the Wrong Way, wherein Men Transgress the Rules of Honesty, Proven an Hard Way. And the Good Way of Religion therefore Preferred & Commended. In a Lecture at Boston, on a Special & Mournful Occasion. *pp.* 46.
Sm. 8° *Boston,* 1712.

The Wayes and Joyes of Early Piety. One Essay More, To Describe and Commend A Walk in the Truth Of our Great Saviour, Unto the Children of His People. In the Audience of the General Assembly of the Massachusett-Province. By Cotton Mather, D.D. *pp. (2),* 54, *(2), (4).*
12° *Boston in N. E. Printed by B. Green, Sold by Samuel Gerrish,* 1712.

Adversus Libertinos. Or, Evangelical Obedience Described and Demanded; In an Essay To Establish, the Holy Law of The Glorious God Upon The Principles of Justification by the Faith of the Gospel. *pp. (4,) 49, (1).*
8° *Boston: Printed by B. Green, for Samuel Gerrish,* 1713.

The Curbed Sinner. A Discourse Upon the Gracious and Wondrous Restraints Laid by the Providence Of the Glorious God On the Sinful Children of Men, to Withold them from Sinning against Him. Occasioned by a Sentence of Death, passed on a poor Young Man, for the Murder of his Companion. With some Historical Passages referring to that Unhappy Spectacle. *pp. (2), xiv., (64).*
12° *Boston, N. E. Printed by John Allen, for Nicholas Boone,* 1713.

A sermon preached after the condemnation of David Wallis.

A Man of his Word. A very brief Essay, on Fidelity In Keeping of Promises and Engagements. Boston-Lecture; in the Audience of his Excellency the Governour, and of the General Assembly 11 d. 4 m. 1713. *pp. (2),* 22.
8° *Boston: Printed by John Allen for N. Boone,* 1713.

A New Offer to the Lovers of Religion and Learning. *pp.* 16.
Sm. 8° *Boston,* 1713.

The Prospectus of Cotton Mather's "Biblia Americana."

A Present of Summer-Fruit. A very brief Essay To Offer Some Instructions of Piety, Which the Summer-Season more Particularly and Emphatically Leads us to; But such also as are never out of Season. Being The short Entertainment of an Auditory in Boston, on a Day distinguished with the Heat of the Summer; 5d. 5m., 1713. *pp. (2),* 29.
12° *Boston: Printed and Sold by B. Green,* 1713.

The Will of a Father Submitted to. The Duty of Patient Submission to every Condition, which the Providence of God, Orders for the Children of Men. Enforced from the Glorious Pattern of the Blessed Jesus, Readily and Cheerfully Submitting to take the Cup, which His Father Had given Him. In a very Brief Discourse, made with a special Regard unto a Religious Family, Burying an Only Son, And at a Time of Much Affliction in the Neighborhood. *pp.* 40.
Sm. 8° *Boston: Printed by Thomas Fleet, for Daniel Henchman,* 1713.

Family-Religion, Excited and Assisted. Also translated into the Massachusetts Indian language. *pp.* 20.
16° *Boston: Printed by B. Green,* 1714.

The Glorious Throne. A Short View of Our Great Lord-Redeemer, on His Throne. Ordering by His Providence all the Changes in the World: and most Particularly, what has Occurred in the Death of Our

6

Late Memorable Sovereign, and the Legal Succession of the British Crown to the Illustrious House of Hanover. In a Sermon on that Great Occasion at Boston in New-England, on 23 d. VII m. 1714. *pp. (2), 37.*
8° *Boston: Printed by B. Green,* 1714.

A Monitor for Communicants. An Essay to Excite and Assist Religious Approaches to the Table of the Lord. Offered by an Assembly of the New English Pastors, unto their own Flocks, and unto all the Churches in these American Colonies : With a Solemn Testimony to the Cause of God, and Religion, in them. *pp.* 21.
12° *Boston: Printed by B. Green,* 1714.

Pascentius : A very Brief Essay upon The Methods of Piety. Wherein People in whom the Difficulties of the Times have caused Anxieties may have a Comfortable Assurance of being at all Times Comfortably Provided for. Offered unto the Inhabitants of Boston, at their Lecture 23. d. x m., 1714. By C. Mather, D.D. & F. R. S. *pp. (2),* 38.
18° *Boston in N. E.: Printed by B. Green, for Benj. Eliot and Joanna Perry,* 1714.

A Perfect Recovery. The Voice of the Glorious God unto persons whom his mercy has recovered from Sickness Exhibited. A Brief Discourse to the Inhabitants of a Place that had passed thro' a very Sickly Winter, and a Time of much Adversity. With Some Remarks on the Shining Patterns of Piety. *pp.* 60.   12° *Boston,* 1714.

Nuncia Bonae Terra Longinqua. A Brief Account of some Good & Great Things a doing For the Kingdom of God, In the Midst of Europe. Communicated in a Letter to —— From Cotton Mather, D.D. & F. R. S. *pp. (2),* 14.
8° *Boston in New-England: Printed by B. Green, for Samuel Gerrish,* 1715.

Shaking Dispensations. An Essay Upon the Mighty Shakes which the Hand of Heaven, hath given, and is giving, to the World. With some Useful Remarks On the Death of the French King, Who left off to make the World a Wilderness, and to destroy the Cities thereof; on the Twenty-first of August. 1715. In a Sermon on that Great Occasion, At Boston, New-England. 13 d. VIII. m. *pp. (2),* 50.
8° *Boston: Printed by B. Green, Sold by S. Gerrish,* 1715.

The Christian Cynick. A brief Essay On a Merciful Saviour. Addressed by an Unworthy Sinner. With Directions and Encouragements For the Addresses, Which will obtain His Favours. *pp. (2),* 42.
12° *Boston,* 1716.

The City of Refuge. The Gospel of the City Explained; And the Flight of a Distressed Sinner Thereunto, Directed and Quickened; With a special Aspect on the Intentions. Early Piety. *pp.* 33.
12° *Boston: Printed by T. Fleet and T. Crump, for Daniel Henchman,* 1716.

Fair Dealing between Debtor and Creditor. A very Brief Essay upon The Caution to be used, about coming into Debt, and getting out of it. Offered at Boston-Lecture; 5. d. VI. m. 17 15-16. *pp. (2),* 30.
8° *Boston: Printed by B. Green, for Samuel Gerrish,* 1716.

Real and Vital Religion Served, In the Various and Glorious Intentions of it. With Eight Essays, upon important Subjects which have a Serviceable Aspect upon it. *pp.* 281, 283.   16° *Boston,* 1716.

43

The Stone Cut out of the Mountain. And The Kingdom of God, in Those Maxims of it, that cannot be shaken. Exhibited in the Year, Seventeen Hundred & Sixteen. Latin Title: Lapis e Monte Excisus. Atque Regnum Dei, Ejusdemque Principia in æternum Stabilienda. 14 leaves. Sm. 8°. Editur Anno Domini, M DCC XVI.

A treatise in English and Latin.

Hades Look'd into. The Power of Our Great Saviour Over the Invisible World, and the Gates of Death which lead into that World. Considered, In A Sermon Preached at the Funeral of the Honourable, Wait Winthrop Esq; Who Expired, 7 d. IX m. 1717. In the LXXVI Year of his Age. *pp.* (2), vi, 46.
8° *Boston, Printed by T. Crump,* 1717.

The preface is by Increase Mather.

Malachi: Or the Everlasting Gospel, preached unto the Nations. And those Maxims of Piety, which are to be the Glorious Rules of Behaviour. The only Terms of Communion, and the Happy Steps to Controversy, among all that Moved, Meet and Serve those Advances which the Kingdom of God is Now Making in the World. *pp.* (2), 93.
Sm. 8° *Boston, Printed by T. Crump for Robert Starke,* 1717.

The Valley of Baca. The Divine Sov'reignty, Displayed and Adored; More Particularly, in Bereaving Dispensations, of the Divine Providence. A Sermon Preached on the Death of Mrs. Hannah Sewall, The Religious & Honourable Consort of Samuel Sewall, Esq; Which befell us, on the 19 d. VIII m. 1717. In the SIXTIETH Year of her Age. *pp.* (2) 28. Sm. 8° *Boston, Printed by B. Green,* 1717.

Victorina, The Pleasures of True Piety, A Sermon Preach'd, On the Decease and At the Desire, of Mrs. Katharin Mather, By her Father. Whereunto there is added, A further Account of that Young Gentlewoman, By another Hand. *pp.* (2), viii, 86.
24° *Boston, Printed by B. Green, for Daniel Henchman,* 1717.

Zelotes. A Zeal For the House of God, Blown up, in a Sermon unto an Assembly of Christians; in the South-Part of Boston on 8 d. xi m. 1716-17. A Day of Prayer Kept by them, at their First Entrance into a New Edifice Erected by them, for the Publick Worship of God our Saviour. *pp.* 44.
12° *Boston, Printed by J. Allen for Nicholas Boone, at the sign of the Bible in Cornhill,* 1717.

Faith Encouraged. A Brief Relation of a Strange Impression from Heaven, on the Minds of some Jewish Children, at the City of Berlin, (in the Upper Saxony). And some Remarks, for the Improvement of so Marvellous an Occurrence. *pp.* 32.
Sm. 8° *Boston, Printed by J. Allen, for T. Fleet,* 1718.

Psalterium Americanum. The Book of Psalms, In a Translation Exactly conformed unto the Original; but all in Blank Verse, Fitted unto Tunes commonly used in our Churches. Which Pure Offering is accompanied with Illustrations, digging for Hidden Treasures in it; And Rules to Employ it upon the Glorious and Various Intentions of it, Whereto are added, Some other Portions of the Sacred Scripture, to Enrich the Cantional. *pp.* (2), xxxv, (1), 426.
Sm. 8° *Boston, in N. E., Printed by S Kneeland, for B. Eliot, S. Gerrish, D. Henchman, and J. Edwards, and Sold at their Shops,* 1718.

"In this singular publication, which is a close translation of the Hebrew, Dr. Mather has not only disregarded the modern practice of breaking the lines, whether rhymed or not, but he has run out (to use a printer's phrase) the whole matter; so that while each psalm looks exactly like prose, and may be read as such, it is, in fact, modulated so that it may be sung as lyric verse. The learned Doctor says that in the 'twice seven versions' which he has seen, the authors 'put in as large an Heap of poor Things. which, are intirely their own,—merely for the sake of preserving the *Clink* of the *Rhyme ;* Which after all is of small consequence unto a Generous Poem; and of none at all unto the Melody of Singing.'"

Mirabilia Dei. An Essay On the very Seasonable & Remarkable Inter-positions of the Divine Providence, To Rescue & Relieve Distressed People, Brought unto the very Point of Perishing; Especially relating to that Twice-Memorable Fifth of November. Offered in the Audi-ence of His Excellency the Governour and the General Assembly of the Massachusetts-Province, New-England, On the Fifth of Novem-ber. 1719. By Cotton Mather, DD. & F.R.S. *pp.* (2), 34.
    8° *Boston, Printed by B. Green, Printer to His Excellency the Governour & Council,* 1719.

The Religion of an Oath. Plain Directions How the Duty of Swear-ing, May be Safely Managed, When it is Justly Demanded. And Strong Persuasives To avoid the Perils of Perjury. Concluding with a most Solemn Explanation of an Oath, which the Laws of Denmark have provided for the consideration of them, whom an Oath is pro-pos'd unto. Published at the Desire of Some, who apprehended Oaths to be too frequently and faultily trifled with. *pp.* (2), 30.
    Sm. 8° *Boston, N. E., Printed by B. Green, for D. Henchman,* 1719.

A Testimony against Evil Customs. Given by Several Minister. *pp.* 4.
    4° *Boston, N. E. Printed by Samuel Kneeland,* 1719.
    Signed by Cotton Mather, Benjamin Wadsworth and Benjamin Colman.

The Tryed Professor. A very Brief Essay, to Detect and Prevent Hypocrisy, and make sure of Sincerity, in the Profession of Religion. A Plain, Short, and Useful Manual for the Self-Examination which every Christian has Frequent and Solemn Occasion for. *pp.* 16.
    Sm. 8° *Boston, in N. E., Printed by S. Kneeland,* 1719.

Coheleth. A Soul upon Recollection; Coming into Incontestible Senti-ments of Religion: Such as all the Sons of Wisdom will and must forever Justify. Written by a Fellow of the Royal Society. Offering the Advice of a Father going out of the World, unto a Son coming into it. *pp.* (2), 46.
    12° *Boston, Printed by S. Kneeland, for S. Gerrish,* 1720.

The Right Way to Shake off a Viper. An Essay upon a Case Too com-monly calling for Consideration: What shall Good Men do, when they are Evil Spoken of? With a Preface of Dr. Increase Mather. The Second Impression. *pp.* (35), xi.   · 12° *S. Kneeland,* 1720.

The Accomplished Singer. Instructions How the Piety of Singing with a True Devotion, may be obtained and expressed; the Glorious God after an uncommon manner Glorified in it, and His People Edified. Intended for the Assistance of all that would sing Psalms with Grace in their Hearts; But more particularly to accompany the Laudable Endeavours of those who are Learning to Sing by Rule, and seeking to preserve a Regular Singing in the Assemblies of the Faithful. *pp.* (4), 24.   16° *Boston, Printed by B. Green, for S. Gerrish,* 1721.
    With an Attestation from Increase Mather.
    One of the rarest of Cotton Mather's tracts; Mather remarks: "It has been found in some of our congregations, that in length of time,

their singing has degenerated into an odd noise, that has had more of what we want a name for than any regular singing in it; whereby the Celestial Exercise is dishonoured; and indeed the Third Commandment is trespassed upon."

The Christian Philosopher: A Collection of the Best Discoveries in Nature, with Religious Improvements. By Cotton Mather, D.D. And Fellow of the Royal Society. *pp.* vii, (1), 304.
8° *London, Eman. Matthews,* M.DCC.XXI.

Honesta Parsimonia; Or, Time Spent as it should be. Proposals, To prevent that Great Folly and Mischief, The Loss of Time; And Employ the Talent of Time So Watchfully and Fruitfully that a Good Account may at Last be given of it. *pp.* (4), 23.
12° *Boston, Printed by S. Kneeland, for J. Edwards,* 1721.

India Christiana. A Discourse, Delivered unto the Commissioners, for the Propagation of the Gospel among the American Indians. Which is Accompanied with several Instruments relating to the Glorious Design of Propagating our Holy Religion, in the Eastern as well as the Western, Indies. An Entertainment which they that are Waiting for the Kingdom of God will receive as Good News from a far Country. By Cotton Mather, D.D. and F.R.S. *pp.* (2), li, 94, (1).
Sm. 8° *Boston, in New-England, Printed by B. Green,* 1721.

Partly in the Indian language of New England. The " Corrigenda," at the end, is usually wanting.

Tremenda. The Dreadful Sound with which The Wicked are to be Thunderstruck. In a Sermon Delivered unto a great Assembly, in which was present, a Miserable African, just going to be Executed, for a most Inhumane and Uncommon Murder, at Boston, May 25th, 1721, To which is added A Conference between a Minister and the Prisoner, on the Day before his Execution. *pp.* 40.
8° *Boston, Printed by B. Green,* 1721.

A Vision in the Temple. The Lord of Hosts Adored; and the Kings of Glory Proclaimed; On a Day of Prayer kept May 10, 1721 at the Opening of the New Brick Meeting House in the North part of Boston, by the Ministers of the City, with the Society which Built it, and this Day Swarmed into it. *pp.* (2), 45.
12° *Boston, Robert Starkey,* 1721.

What the Pious Parent wishes for. By Dr. Cotton Mather. Boston Lecture 23 d. 1 m. 1721. *pp.* 34.
8° *Boston,* 1721.

This is the first sermon in " A Course of Sermons."

The Angel of Bethesda, Visiting the Invalids of a Miserable World. By a Fellow of the Royal Society. *pp.* (2), 17, (1).
8° *New-London, Timothy Green,* 1722.

Love Triumphant. A Sermon at the Gathering of a New Church, And the Ordaining Of their Pastor; In the North Part of Boston; May 23, 1722. With Copies of other Things Offered in the Publick Actions of that Solemn Occasion. *pp.* (4), 39.
Sm. 8° *Printed by S. Kneeland, for Nath. Belknap,* 1722.

The Minister. A Sermon, Offer'd unto the Anniversary Convention of Ministers, From several Parts of New-England, Met at Boston, 31 d. 3 m. 1722. By One of their Number. And published at the Request of them that heard it. *pp.* (2), 45.
8° *Boston, Printed in the Year* 1722.

The half-title is "Dr. Cotton Mather's Sermon at the Anniversary Convention."

The Soul upon the Wing. An Essay on The State of the Dead. Answering That Solemn Enquiry, How the Children of Men are at their Death disposed of? In a Sermon Occasion'd by the Decease of some Desirable Friends lately Departed. By One of the Ministers in the North-part of Boston. *pp.* (4), 24.
8° *Boston, N. E. Printed by B. Green,* 1722.

The Converted Sinner. The Nature of a Conversion to Real and Vital Piety. And the Manner in which it is to he Pray'd & Striv'n for A Sermon preached in Boston, May 31, 1724. In the Hearing of certain Pirates, a little before their Execution. *pp. (4),* 49.
8° *Boston: Printed for Nath'l Belknap,* 1722.

"These pirates, John Rose Areder and William White, executed June 2, 1724, belonged to the crew of the dreaded John Phillips." *See* Drake's 'History of Boston,' p. 570.—J. H. TRUMBULL.

Cœlestinus. A Conversation in Heaven, Quickened and Assisted, with Discoveries of Things in the Heavenly World. And some Relations of the Views and Joys That have been granted unto Several Persons in the Confines of it. Introduced by Agathangelus, Or, An Essay on the Ministry of the Holy Angels. And Recommended unto the People of God, by the very Reverend Dr. Increase Mather; Waiting in the Daily Expectation of his Departure to that Glorious World. *pp.* (2), viii, 27, ii, 162.
12° *Boston, Printed by S. Kneeland, for Nath. Belknap,* 1723.

Published by Dr. Cotton Mather, with a dedication to Mr. Thomas Hollis.

Euthanasia. A Sudden Death Made Happy and Easy to the Dying Believer. Exemplified in John Frizell, Esq; Who so Expired, April 10, 1723. *pp.* (4), 27. 8° *Boston, Printed by S. Kneeland,* MDCCXXIII.

The Voice of God in a Tempest. A Sermon Preached in the Time of the Storm; Wherein many and heavy and unknown Losses were Suffered at Boston, (and Parts Adjacent,) Febr. 24, 1722-3. By one of the Ministers in Boston. *pp.* (4), 19.
12° *Boston, N. E., Printed by S. Kneeland,* MDCCXXIII.

The Nightingale. An Essay on Songs among Thorns. Or the Supports & Comforts of the Afflicted Believer. Thankfully Published by One that has had Experience of them. *pp. (4),* 19.
8° *Boston in New England: Printed by B. Green,* 1724.

Parentator. Memoirs of Remarkables in the Life and the Death of the Ever-Memorable Dr. Increase Mather. Who Expired, August 23, 1723. *pp. (2), x., xiv.,* 239, *(6).*
Sm. 8° *Boston: Printed by B. Green, for Nathaniel Belknap,* 1724.

Rewritten and issued as "Memoirs of the Life of the late Reverend Increase Mather."

Christodulus. A Good Reward of A Good Servant. Or, The Service of a Glorious Christ, Justly Demanded and Commended, from a View of the Glory with which it shall be Recompensed [*sic*]. With Some Commemoration of Mr. Thomas Walter, Lately a Pastor to a Church in Roxbury: Who had an Early Dismission from what of that Service was to be done in This World. Jan. 10, 1724-5. By Cotton Mather, D.D. and F. R. S. *pp. (3), iii,* 33.
8° *Boston: Printed by T. Fleet, for S. Gerrish,* 1725.

The Rev. Thomas Walter was a grandson of Increase and a nephew of Cotton Mather.

The Palm-Bearers. A brief Relation of Patient and Joyful Sufferings; and of Death Gloriously Triumphed over; In the History of the Persecution which the Church of Scotland suffered, from the Year 1660, to the Year 1668. *pp. (2), viii.,* 58.
Sm. 8° *Boston: Printed by T. Fleet, for S. Gerrish,* 1725.

Vital Christianity: A brief Essay On the Life of God, in the Soul of Man; Produced and Maintained by a Christ Living in us: and The Mystery of a Christ within, Explained. *pp. (4),* 30.
8° *Printed by Samuel Keimer, for Eleazer Phillips, in Charles-Town in New-England,* 1725.

Ecclesiæ Manilia. The Peculiar Treasure of the Almighty King opened: And the Jewels that are made up in Exposed. At Boston Lecture, July 14, 1726. Whereof ONE is more particularly Exhibited, in the Character of Mrs. Elizabeth Cotton, Who was Laid up a few Days before. And Certain Instruments and Memorials of Piety, Written by that Valuable and Honourable Gentlewoman. *pp. (2),* 42.
8° *Boston: Daniel Henchman,* 1726.

Mrs. Cotton was the widow of Rev. Roland Cotton, of Sandwich, Mass., and a sister of Gurdon Saltonstall, Governor of Connecticut.

A Good Old Age. A Brief Essay on The Glory of Aged Piety. Humbly Commended and Presented unto Them whose Arrival to, or near, Sixty, ranks them Among The Aged. *pp. (2),* 42.
Sm. 8° *Boston: Printed by S. Kneeland and T. Green, for S. Gerrish,* · 1726.

Hatzar-Maveth. Comfortable Words; In a Short Essay on the Comforts Of One Living to God, but Walking through the Valley of the Shadow of Death, and finding it no more than A Shadow of Death. *pp. (4),* 28. 12° *Boston,* 1726.

Manuductio ad Ministerium. Directions for a Candidate of the Ministry. Wherein, First, a Right Foundation is laid for his Future Improvement; And, Then, Rules are Offered for such a Management of his Academical & Preparatory Studies; And thereupon, For such a Conduct after his Appearance in the World; as May Render him a Skilful and Useful Minister of the Gospel. *pp. (2), xviii, (2),* 151.
8° *Boston: Printed for Thomas Hancock,* 1726.

Nails Fastened. Or, Proposals of Piety Reasonably and Seasonably Complyed withal. A Brief Essay on the Conduct Expected of such as have had their Duty Proposed unto them. Designed more Particularly to be Lodg'd and Left, where Pastoral Visits, have Watched for the Souls of a Gospellized People. *pp. (2),* 22.
12° *Boston: Joseph Edwards,* MDCCXXVI.

Ratio Disciplinæ Fratrum Nov-Anglorum. A Faithful Account of the Discipline Professed and Practised; in the Churches of New-England. With Interspersed and Instructive Reflections on the Discipline of the Primitive Churches. *pp. (2), iv.,* 207, *(3).*
Sm. 8° *Boston: S. Gerrish,* 1726.

In a postscript, on page 208, Cotton Mather owns himself the author of this book, a sort of historical relation of the church discipline of New England. Preceding is an attestation of four pages, dated the 10th Oct. 1719, and signed by Increase Mather.

Suspiria Vinctorum. Some Account of the Condition to which the Protestant Interest in the World is at This Day reduced. And the

Duty, to which all that would prove themselves True Christians must and will count themselves obliged. *pp. (2), 22.*
12° *Boston: Printed by T. Fleet,* 1726.

The Balance of the Sanctuary. A Short and Plain Essay; Declaring The True Balance Wherein Every Thing Should be Weighed, And Detecting, The False Balance. A Lecture. In the Audience of the General Assembly at Boston, Oct. 5, 1727. *pp. (2), 24.*
12° *Boston: Printed by T. Fleet,* 1727.

Christian Loyalty. Or, Some Suitable Sentiments On the Withdraw of King George the First, Of Glorious Memory, And the Access of King George the Second, Unto the Throne of the British Empire. By Cotton Mather. *pp. (2), ii., 25.*
16° *Boston; Printed by T. Fleet,* 1727.

Hor-Hagidgad. An Essay upon, An Happy Departure. Occasioned By the Decease of the Valuable Mr. William Waldron, Late Pastor to one of the Churches in Boston; Who Departed, Sept. 11, 1727. By Cotton Mather, D.D. and F.R.S. *pp. (4), 8, 28.*
8° *Boston: S. Gerrish,* 1727.

Ignorantia Scientifica. A brief Essay on Mans not knowing his Time: The Just Inferences from it, And the Great Advantages of it. Upon a Special and Mournful Occasion. *pp. (4), 24.*
Sm. 8° *Boston in N. E. Printed by B. Green, for Samuel Gerrish,* 1727.

The Marrow of the Gospel. A very brief Essay, on the Union Between the Redeemer And the Beleever. *pp. 24.*
8° *Boston: N. Belknap,* 1727.

The Terror of the Lord. Some Account of the Earthquake That shook New-England, In the Night, Between the 29 and the 30 of October. 1727. With a Speech, Made Unto the Inhabitants of Boston, Who Assembled the Next Morning, for the proper Exercises of Religion, On so Uncommon, and so Tremendous an Occasion. *pp. (4), 37, 6.*
8° *Boston: Printed by T. Fleet, for S. Kneeland,* 1727.

The Comfortable Chambers, Opened and Visited, upon the Departure of that Aged and Faithful Servant of God, Mr. Peter Thatcher, The Never-to-be-forgotten Pastor of Milton. Who made his flight thither, On December 17, 1727. *pp. (2), 31.*
Sm. 8° *Boston: Printed for J. Edwards,* 1728.

"This was the last Sermon my Father deliver'd from the pulpit: and truly such a Sermon as a good Minister would desire shou'd be his last."—S. MATHER. An obituary of Mr. Thatcher is given in "Addenda from the 'Weekly Journal,' No. XI., Milton, December 23, 1727," *pp. 4.*

The Mystical Marriage. A Brief Essay, on, The Grace of the Redeemer espousing The Soul of the Believer. By the Late Reverend Dr. Cotton Mather. Approved by Several Pastors of our Churches. *pp. (4), 16.*
12° *Boston, N. E.: N. Belknap,* MDCCXXVIII.

The Widow of Naim. Remarks On the Illustrious Miracle Wrought by Our Almighty Redeemer, On the behalf of a Desolate Widow. By the Late Reverend Cotton Mather. *pp. (4), 30.*
8° *Boston: Printed in the Year* MDCCXXVIII.

This was written in 1724, and dedicated to Mrs. Dorothy Frizzel.

A Monitory Letter To them who Needlessly and Frequently Absent themselves from the Publick Worship of GOD. Briefly Representing the Nature and Intent of Religious Assemblies, And the Grievous Evil of Profane Absence from them. *pp. (15), (2).* Second Edition.
12° *Boston: Printed by S. Kneeland & T. Green,* 1738.

Family Religion Excited and Assisted. The third impression.
8° *Newport,* 1740.

The Case of a troubled Mind. A brief Essay, Which apprehends the Face of a Gracious God Hidden from it. The Symptoms of the Troubles, and the Methods of preventing them. The Second Edition. *pp. 23.* 8° *Boston: Printed by G. Rogers, for N. Proctor,* 1741.

Signatus. The Sealed Servants Of our God, Appearing with Two Witnesses, To produce a Well-Established Assurance Of their being the Children of the Lord Almighty. Or The Witness of the Holy Spirit, with the Spirit of the Beleever, to his Adoption of God; briefly and plainly Described. At Boston Lecture, 1726-7. *pp.* VIII. 31.
The Second Edition. With a Preface and Appendix by the Rev. Mr. Croswell. 8° *Boston: Printed by Rogers & Fowle,* 1748.

Essays to do Good. Addressed to all Christians. By the Late Cotton Mather. A New Edition, Improved by George Burder. From the Latest London Edition. *pp. 148.*
12° *Boston: Printed by Lincoln & Edmands,* 1808.

Also an edition published by the American Tract Society, New York.
n. d.

Proposals to Lawyers. From Essays to do Good. *pp. 8.*
8° *Barnard, Vt.: Published by T. Dix,* n. d.

AZARIAH MATHER.

Wo to Sleepy Sinners. Or, A Discourse upon Amos VI. 1. Begun in a Lecture at Saybrook, January 6, 1719, 20. *pp. (2), 29, (1).*
8° *New London: Printed by T. Green,* 1720.

None but Christ. A Discourse on John VI. 67, 68. Preach'd Privately, to a Religious Society in Say-brook. *pp. (2), 22.*
8° *New London: T. Green,* 1722.

The Sabbath-Day's Rest Asserted, Explained, Proved, and Applied. *pp. (2), 4, 38, (1).*
8° *Boston, N. E. Printed by B. Green, Jun., for S. Gerrish,* 1725.

"An Attestation," pp. 4, is signed "Co. Mather."

Good Rulers a choice Blessing. A Sermon preached before the Great and General Assembly of the Colony of Connecticut, at Hartford, in New-England, May 12th, 1725. The Day for the Election of the Honourable the Governour & Deputy-Governour and the Worshipful Assistants there. By Azariah Mather, A. M., Pastor of Christ's Church in Saybrook. Published (with the addition of some things either not Delivered at the Preaching, though Written; or but hinted) by Order of Authority. *pp. (2), 49, 1.*
8° *New London: T. Green,* 1725.

7

SAMUEL MATHER (OF BOSTON).

De Ordinatione Dissertatio Historica. *pp.* 46.   *Londini*, MDCCXIII.

A Discourse Concerning the Necessity of Believing the Doctrine of the Holy Trinity as profess'd and maintain'd by the Established Church of England. . . . *pp.* (3), 75, 1.   . 4° *London,* 1719.

A Discourse Concerning the God Head of the Holy Ghost, The Third Person in the Eternal Trinity Wherein the Sentiments of Dr. Clarke are considered. *pp.* (viii), 141, 2.   4° *London,* 1719.

An Essay Concerning Gratitude. Written by Samuel Mather, M.A. and Chaplain to his Majesty's Castle William. *pp.* (7), 53.
Boston, N. E., Printed for T. Hancock, MDCCXXII.

The Departure and Character of Elijah Considered and Improved. A Sermon After the Decease of the very Reverend and Learned Cotton Mather, D.D., F. R. S. and Minister of the North Church, who expired Feby. 13, 1727-8. In the Sixty-sixth Year of his Age. *pp.* 4, 26.
8° *Boston: Printed by G. Rogers,* 1728.

The Life of the Very Reverend and Learned Cotton Mather, D. D. & F. R. S. Late Pastor of the North Church in Boston. Who Died, Feby. 13, 1727-8. *pp.* (4), iv, 6, 10, 186.   8° *Boston,* MDCCXXIX.

An Essay Concerning Gratitude. Written by Samuel Mather, A. M., and Chaplain to His Majesty's Castle William. *pp.* 53.
8° *Boston, Printed for T. Hancock,* MDCCXXXII.

All Men Will not be Saved Forever or an Attempt to prove That this is a Scriptural Doctrine; and To give a sufficient Answer to the Publisher of Extracts in Favor of the Salvation of All Men, &c. *pp.* 31.
8° *Boston, Printed by Benjamin Edes,* MDCCLXXXII.
    Second Edition, pp. 32, MDCCLXXXIII.

An Apology for the Liberties of the Churches in New England, to which is prefix'd a Discourse concerning Congregational Churches. *pp.* 216.
8° *Boston, Printed by T. Fleet,* 1738.

The Fall of the Mighty lamented. A Funeral Discourse Upon the Death of Her Most Gracious Majesty Wilhelmina Dorothea Carolina, Queen Consort to His Majesty of Great Britain, France and Ireland: Preached on March 23, 1737-8, In the Audience of His Excellency the Governour the honourable the Lieutenant-Governour, and the honourable His Majesty's Council at the Thursday Lecture in Boston, New-England. *pp.* (2), 33.   8° *Boston, Printed by J. Draper,* 1738.

War is lawful, and Arms are to be proved. A Sermon Preached to the Ancient and Honourable Artillery Company, on June 4, 1739. The Anniversary Day for Electing their Officers, at Boston, New-England. *pp.* 33.   8° *Boston, Printed by T. Fleet,* 1739.

The Faithful Man abounding with Blessings. A Funeral Discourse Upon the Death of the Honourable Thomas Hutchinson, Esq.; one of His Majesty's Council for the Province of the Massachusetts-Bay in New-England; who Departed this Life on December 3, 1739. *pp.* (2), 32.   8° *Boston, Printed by J. Draper,* MDCCXL.

A Funeral Discourse Preached on the Occasion of the Death of The High, Puissant and most Illustrious Prince Frederick Lewis, Prince of Great Britain, Electoral Prince of Brunswick-Lunenburgh, Prince of Wales, Duke of Cornwall, &c. In the Audience of the Honerable

Spencer Phips, Esq.; Lieutenant-Governor and Commander in Chief; and the Honorable Council, of the Province of the Massachusetts-Bay; On May 22d, 1751, at Boston, New-England. *pp.* 31.
8° *Boston, Printed by John Draper,* 1751.

The Walk of the Upright with its Comfort. A Funeral Discourse after the Decease of the Rev. William Welsted who died April 29, and Mr. Ellis Gray, who died on January 7th preceeding it. Colleague Pastors of a Church in Boston. Preached to their People in the New Brick Meeting-House, on May 6, 1753. *pp.* 34.
8° *Boston, for Michael Dennis,* 1753.

A Dissertation Concerning the Most remarkable name of Jehovah. *pp.* 101.   8° *Boston,* 1760.

Of the Pastoral Care: A Sermon Preached to the Reverend Ministers of the Province of the Massachusetts-Bay in New-England, at their Annual Convention in Boston, on May 27, 1762. By Samuel Mather, M. A. *pp.* 31.   8° *Boston, Printed by Thomas and John Fleet,* 1762.

Essay on the Lord's Prayer (half title). The Lord's Prayer or a new attempt to recover the *right version* and *genuine Meaning* of that Prayer. *pp.* iv, 66, 1.
8° *Boston, Printed by Kneeland & Adams,* MDCCLXVI.

An Attempt to shew, that America must be Known to the Ancients; made at the Request, and to gratify the Curiosity of an Inquisitive Gentleman: To which is added an Appendix concerning the American Colonies, and some Modern Managements against them. By an American Englishman, Pastor of a Church in Boston. *pp.* 35.
8° *Boston, J. Kneeland,* 1773.

The preface, which comes before the title page, is signed by Samuel Mather, the Author.

The Dying Legacy of an Aged Minister of the Everlasting Gospel, to the United States of North America. *pp. (2),* 11, 29.
8° *Boston, Printed by Benjamin Edes and Sons, in Cornhill,*
M,DCC,LXXXIII.

Account of the first Settlement of Boston, written in the Year 1784, by the late Dr. Samuel Mather. Mass. Historical Society Collections, page 256,   1792.

MOSES MATHER.

Sermon Preached in the Audience of the General Assembly of the State of Connecticut, in Hartford, on the Day of their Anniversary Election, May 10, 1781.
New London: Printed by Timothy Green, Printer to the Governor and Company,   M.DCCLXXXI.

MATHER MANUSCRIPTS.

In addition to printed works of the Mather family in the library of the Society, there is also a large and valuable collection of their manuscripts, including treatises, sermons, diaries, interleaved almanacs, letters and memoranda. It would require much more time to prepare a complete catalogue of this interesting matter than the compiler can give to it; he must therefore content himself with a few of the more important titles.

In the hand-writing of Richard Mather is the original draft of the Cambridge Platform. Also

"Answer of the Elders to certaine doubts and objections against sundry passages in ye platform of Discipline agreed upon by ye late Synod." (Oct. 26, 1635.)

"Answers to Arguments for the Government of the Church to be in the hands of the People." 1644.

"Observations and Arguments respecting the Government of Christian Churches." 1650.

"Answers to twenty-one questions from the General Court at Hartford to the General Court at Boston. 1657."

Of Increase Mather's may be mentioned his Auto-biography, written for his children.

"Testimony against Several profane and superstitious customs prevalent in New-England."

(This was printed in 1687.)

"Sermons for the Sacrament." 1713—1719.

Interleaved Almanacs, with manuscript notes, from 1660 to 1721, also sermons and letters.

In the hand-writing of Cotton Mather, are a large number of treatises, sermons, letters, diaries and memoranda. Of these the following are probably of the most interest:

"A Brand Pluck'd out of the Burning."

This is an account of Mercy Short who suffered from Witchcraft, of whom mention is made in " Another Brand Pluck't out of the Burning, or, More Wonders of the Invisible World."

" The Angel of Bethesda, or some Remarks on the grand Cause of Sickness." (This was printed in 1722).

" The Best of Blessings,—Real and Vital Piety defended and assisted in six brief essays, &c."

"The Lord in the Garden."

"Yᵉ Lord Before the Ecclesiastical Court."

"Yᵉ Lord Before the Political Court."

" One Among the Myrtle trees. A Brief & plain Essay on Good Services to be done by people in low stations."

" The New Heavens Opened."

" Where to find Gog and Magog."

" The New Earth Surveyed."

"When shall those things be? When the Grand Revolution to be look'd for!"

" The Ancient Gospel." 26 d. 6 m. 1688.

Five "Sacramental Discourses on the name of yᵉ Lord Jesus Christ." 1689.

"A Day of Prayer Kept by the North Church for Discussion about yᵉ calling of a Minister." 2 d. 8 m. 1717.

"Triparadisus. Essays on, I. The paradise of the old world enriched with some instructive illustrations on the Sacred Geography. II. The Paradise of Departed Spirits fortifyed with well attested Relations to demonstrate as well as illustrate the state of such. III. The Paradise of the New Earth under the influences of the New Heavens."

" A Discourse concerning Congregational Churches."

"The Observations and Reflections of the Rev. Dr. Cotton Mather concerning Witchcraft. 1692."

" A Declaration of the Oppressed Bretheren in the South part of Boston."

"Letter to the Bretheren of the Church at New Haven, 20th 4 m. 1715."

" Letter proposing an address to the New King." (Geo. I).

" Letter respecting the appointing of a Chaplain at the Castle." Nov. 7, 1716.

"Letter concerning the call of Mr. Fisk to the New South Church, Boston."

Among the manuscripts of Samuel Mather of Boston, are:

"Disquisition concerning the most Holy Duty in which it is endeavoured to communicate the Scriptural Doctrine concerning God, and His Manifestation to His Intelligent Creatures, &c. In 12 chapters."

The Song. The Very Songs. To Shelomoh, or Solomon himself, the Prince of Peace: or An Honest Attempt to translate and explain the same with desirable Truth & Fidelity."

"Scriptural Philosophy. An Attempt to show That the Right Principles of Natural Philosophy are contained in the Sacred Writings. By one of the Academy of Arts and Sciences in the Massachusetts Commonwealth."

ADDENDA.

SINCE the "List of Books" was printed, the second part of the Brinley Library has been sold in New York, the auction occurring March 22, 1880, and the three following days. At this sale, the Antiquarian Society had a credit of $1250 in addition to a small balance from the credit at the first, enabling them to add to their collections one hundred and ninety-two books, and one hundred and fourteen pamphlets.

Among the more important works received were the following :— .

Byfield (Nathaniel). An account of the Late Revolution in New-England. Together with the Declaration of the Gentlemen, Merchants, and Inhabitants of Boston, and the Country adjacent. *April 18, 1689, pp. 20.* Sm. 4° *London, for Ric. Chiswell,* 1689.
   The first London edition.

Massachusetts. A Copy of the Kings Majesties Charter, for Incorporating the Company of the Massachusets Bay in New-England in America. Granted in the fourth Year of his Highness Reign of England, Scotland, France and Ireland, *Anno Dom.* 1628. Wood-cut of the Massachusetts seal on the title-page. *pp. (2) 26.*
   4° *Boston, S. Green, for B. Harris,* 1689.

[White (Rev. John)]. The Planters Plea. Or The Grovnds of Plantations examined, and vsuall Objections answered. Together with a manifestation of the causes mooving such as have lately undertaken a Plantation in Nevv-England : for the satisfaction of those that question the lawfulnesse of the Action. *pp. (4) 84.*
   4° *London, William Iones,* 1630.

Wood (William). New Englands Prospect. A true, lively, and experimentall description of that part of America, commonly called New-England, &c. *pp. (8), 83, (5).*
   Sm. 4° *London, Tho. Cotes, for John Bellamie,* 1635.

The Charters of the Province of Pensilvania and City of Philadelphia. *pp.* 30. *Philadelphia. B. Franklin*, 1742—Penn and the Indians, *a Magazine article*, 4 *leaves inlaid, n. p., n. d.* 2 *in* 1 *vol., Portrait of Franklin (Cochin*, 1777, *engr. by St. Aubin) inserted; also, engraving of the "remnant of the Great Tree" under which Penn's Treaty with the Indians was made.* Sm. *folio.*

The Pennsylvania Packet and Daily Advertiser: April 14th—Dec. 30th, 1785 (Nos. 1931-2154). *folio, J. Dunlap & D. C. Claypoole.*

M. T. Cicero's Cato Major, or his Discourse of Old-Age: With Explanatory Notes. *pp.* viii, 159, rubricated title.
8° *Philadelphia, B. Franklin*, 1744.

A fine copy, with the autograph of President Thomas Clap, of Yale College, "dono D. Benj. Franklin. 1746." Measures 7⅜ by 4¼ inches.

Gospel Order Revived, Being an Answer to a Book lately set forth by the Reverend Mr. Increase Mather, President of Harvard College, &c. Entituled, *The Order of the Gospel*, &c. By sundry Ministers of the Gospel in New-England. 5 prelim. leaves, *pp.* 40.
4° n. p. [*New York, Wm. Bradford,*] 1700.

For the history of the book. see THOMAS's *Hist. of Printing*, II. 90, and 458-66, and SIBLEY's *Harvard Graduates*, I. 455.

Keith (George.) The Presbyterian and Independent Visible Churches in New-England and Else-where, Brought to the Test,... with a Call and Warning from the Lord to the People of Boston and New-England, to Repent, &c. And two Letters to the Preachers in Boston; and an Answer to the gross Abuses, Lyes and Slanders of Increase Mather and Nath. Morton, &c., 5 prelim. leaves, *pp.* 280.
Sm. 8° *London, Thomas Northcott*, 1691.

Several scarce local histories and valuable volumes relating to the American Revolution were also obtained.

The Mather publications added to the library were as follows:—

Mather (Cotton). Reasonable Religion: or, the Truths of the Christian Religion demonstrated. With the Religion of the Closet, and Family Religion Urged. Preface, by Rev. Dr. [Daniel] Williams, *pp.* (20), 136. 12° *London*, 1713.
From the Boston edition of 1700.

Mather (Cotton). The Wonders of the Invisible World: being an Account of the Tryals of Several Witches, lately executed in New-England: And of several remarkable Curiosities therein Occurring. Together with, I. Observations upon the Nature, the Number, and the Operations of the Devils. II. A short Narrative of a late outrage committed by a knot of Witches in *Swede-Land*, [etc]. III. Some Councels directing a due Improvement of the Terrible things lately done: in New-England. IV. A Brief Discourse upon those *Temptations* which are the more ordinary Devices of Satan. By Cotton Mather. Published by the special command, [etc.]
4° *Printed first, at Boston; repr. at London, for John Dunton*, 1693.

This is the first (and only complete) London edition. The last page (before the leaf of "Advertisements") is numbered 98. but the pagination is irregular. the number of pages being in fact, 106, exclusive of the three preliminary leaves not numbered. The leaf which in some copies precedes the Title, containing a Half-Title, and copy of the "Imprimatur," is wanting.

Mather (Increase). A Further Account of the Tryals of the New-England Witches. To which is added, Cases of Conscience concerning Witchcrafts and Evil Spirits, by Increase Mather, President of Harvard Colledge. (with a Postscript.), *pp.* (2), 10, (4), 39, (5). 4° *London, for John Dunton,* 1693.

The first part of the work (pp. 1-10) is Deodat Lawson's " True Narrative " etc., taken from Cotton Mather's " Wonders of the Invisible World."

Jennings (David). An Abridgment of the Life of the late Reverend and Learned Dr. Cotton Mather... Recommended by I. Watts, D. D., *pp.* xii, (4), 144. 12° *London,* 1744.

A volume, by Samuel Mather, Pastor of the Church at Windsor, Conn., has also been added to the Library, entitled :

Two Discourses by the late Reverend Mr. Samuel Mather, Pastor of the Church at Windsor.—I. A dead Faith anatomized. II. The Self-Justiciary, convicted and condemned. *pp.* (2) 108 (1) 82. 12° *Boston, Re-Printed by J. Draper, for D. Henchman, Cornhill.* MDCCXL.

On page 50 of the list the author of the three first named books should have been stated as Samuel Mather of Witney.

A LIST OF MATHER PUBLICATIONS

ADDED TO THE LIBRARY OF THE

AMERICAN ANTIQUARIAN SOCIETY

FROM APRIL, 1880, TO APRIL, 1887.

THE following list of Mather publications has been prepared by Edmund M. Barton, Librarian of the Society, and includes all titles added to the Library from the Brinley collection and other sources since the publication of the original list by Nathaniel Paine, in 1879, and his ''Addenda," in April, 1880.

References are made to the original ''List" where other editions of the works hereinafter mentioned appear.

AZARIAH MATHER.

A Discourse concerning the Death of the Righteous; Had at Lyme, occasion'd by the decease of the Reverend Mr. Moses Noyes. Who dyed November 10th, 1729. 8° *pp.* (4), 24.
N. London, Printed & Sold by T. Green, 1731.

COTTON MATHER.

MDCLXXXIII. The Boston Ephemeris. An Almanack for the (Dyonisian) Year of the Christian Æra MDCLXXXIII. 12° *pp.* 23.
Boston in New-England Printed by S. G. for S. S. 1683.

Work upon the Ark. Meditations upon the Ark as a Type of the Church; Delivered in a Sermon at Boston, and now Dedicated unto the Service of All, but especially of those whose Concerns Lye in Ships. By Cotton Mather. 8° *pp.* (10), 54.
Boston Printed by Samuel Green, and Sold by Joseph Browning
at the corner of the Prison Lane, 1689.

The Present State of New England. Considered in a Discourse on the Necessities and Advantages of a Public Spirit in every Man; Especially, at such a time as this. Made at the Lecture in Boston 20. d 1. m. 1690. Upon the News of an Invasion by bloody Indians and Frenchmen, begun, upon us. By Cotton Mather. 8° *pp.* (2), 52.
Boston: Printed by Samuel Green, 1690.

Preparatory Meditations upon [S. Lee's] ''The Day of Judgment." By Cotton Mather. 12° *pp.* 36.
Boston in New-England Printed by Bartholomew Green for Nicholas
Buttolph, at the Corner of Gutteridg's Coffee-House. 1692.

Ornaments for the Daughters of Zion. Or the Character and Happiness of a Vertuous [sic] Woman : in a Discourse which Directs the Female-Sex how to Express the Fear of God in every Age and State of their Life; and Obtain both Temporal and Eternal Blessedness. Written by Cotton Mather. 12° *pp.* 104.
Cambridge: Printed by S. G. and B. G. for Samuel Phillips
at Boston, 1692.

Also, third edition, 12° pp. (4), 116. Boston, 1741.

For edition of 1694, see page 33.

The Wonders of the Invisible World. Observations as well Historical as Theological, upon the Nature, the Number, and the Operations of the Devils. . . . . By Cotton Mather. $8^\circ pp.$ (32), 151, (1), 32, (24). *Boston Printed and Sold by Benjamin Harris, for Sam. Phillips.* 1693.
For London edition of the same year, see page 56.

The Life and Death of the Reverend Mr John Eliot, who was the First Preacher of the Gospel to the Indians in America. With an Account of the Wonderful Success which the Gospel has had amongst the Heathen in that Part of the World: And of the many strange Customs of the Pagan Indians in New-England. Written by Cotton Mather. The Third Edition carefully Corrected. $8^\circ pp.$ (8), 168, (4).
London: Printed for John Dunton, at the Raven in the Poultrey.
MDCXCIV.
See page 32 for Second Edition, 1691.

A Good Man Making a Good End. The Life and Death, of the Reverend Mr John Baily, . . . in a Sermon, on the Day of his Funeral, . . . 16d. 10m. 1697. By Cotton Mather. $12^\circ pp.$ 88.
Boston in N. E.: Printed by B. Green 1698.

The Everlasting Gospel. The Gospel of Justification by the Righteousness of God, As 'tis Held and Preach'd in the Churches of New-England: Expressed in a Brief Discourse on that Important Article; made at Boston in the year, 1699, by Cotton Mather. $12^\circ pp.$ (32), 76.
Boston: Printed by B. Green, and J. Allen, for Nicholas Buttolph. 1700.

The Good Old Way. Or Christianity Described, From the Glorious Lustre of it, Appearing in the Lives of the Primitive Christians. An Essay tending, from Illustrious Examples of a Sober, & a Righteous, and a Godly Life, Occurring in the Ancient Church-History, to Revive the Languishing Interests of Genuine and Practical Christianity. $12^\circ pp.$ (2), 94.
Boston: Printed by B. Green, for Benj. Eliot at his Shop under the West-End of the Town-House. 1706.

The Day which the Lord hath made. A Discourse concerning the Institution and Observation of the Lords-Day. Delivered in a Lecture, at Boston 4d. 1m. 1703. $8^\circ pp.$ (2), 36, (2).
Boston, N. E. Re-printed by B. Green. 1707.
With an Indian translation by Rev. Samuel Danforth.

A Very Needful Caution. A Brief Essay, to discover the Sin that Slayes its Ten Thousands; And Represent the Character and Condition of the Coveteous. With some Antidotes against the Infection of Coveteousness and Earthly-Mindedness. $12^\circ pp.$ 60.
Boston in N. E. Printed and Sold by Timothy Green. 1707.

Winthropi Justa. A Sermon at the Funeral of the Honble John Winthrop, Esq. Late Governour of the Colony of Connecticut in New-England. Who Died at Boston Nov. 27 1707. in his 69th Year. By Cotton Mather. $12^\circ pp.$ (4), 40.
Boston 1708.
See page 40 for London edition of 1710.

Just Commemorations. The Death of Good Men, Considered; and the Characters of Some who have lately Died in the Service of the Churches, Exhibited. Unto which is added, a Brief Account of the Evangelical Work among the Christianized Indians of New England; Whereof One of the Persons here Commemorated, was a Valuable and Memorable Instrument. $8^\circ pp.$ (2) liv, 58.
Boston in N. E. Printed by B. Green. [1715.]

A Sorrowful Spectacle. In Two Sermons. Occasioned by a Just Sentence of Death, on a Woman, . . . for the Murder of a Spurious Offspring. With some Remarkable Things, relating to the Criminal; proper for All to be informed of. By Cotton Mather. $12°$ pp. (2) vii. 3–92.
Boston: Printed by T. Fleet & T. Crump, for Samuel Gerrish. 1715.

The Echo's of Devotion. A very brief and plain Essay on those Acts of Compliance which all Calls to Piety, are to be Entertained withal. More particularly, the most Edifying Way both of Reading the Scripture, and of Hearing a Sermon, Proposed and Commended. . . . . . $12°$ pp. 36.
Boston: Printed by T. Fleet & T. Crump, for Samuel Gerrish. 1716.

Vigilius. Or the Awakener, Making a Brief Essay, to Rebuke first the Natural Sleep Which too often proves a Dead Fly, in the Devotions of them that indulge it. And then the Moral Sleep, Wherein the Souls of Men frequently Omit the Duties, and Forfeit the Comforts of Religion in Earnest. $8°$ pp. (2), 14.
Boston: Printed by J. Franklin. 1719.

Detur Digniori. The Righteous Man described & asserted as the Excellent Man; And the Excellencies of such an One demonstrated. In a Sermon, upon the Death of the Reverend Mr Joseph Gerrish, late Pastor to the Church in Wenham. . . . . . $12°$ pp. (2), 29.
Boston: Printed by B. Green. 1720.

Terra Beata. A Brief Essay, on the Blessing of Abraham; Even the Grand Blessing of a Glorious Redeemer. $12°$ pp. (2), 54.
Boston: J. Phillips. MDCCXXVI.

A Father Departing. A Sermon on the Departure of the Venerable and Memorable Dr. Increase Mather, who Expired Aug. 23, 1723. In the Eighty-fifth Year of his Age. By One who, as a Son with a Father, served with him in the Gospel. $8°$ pp. 31.
Boston: Printed by T. Fleet, for N. Belknap, at his Shop near Scarlet's Wharf. 1723.

The Comfortable Chambers, Opened and Visited, upon the Departure of that Aged and Faithful Servant of God, Mr. Peter Thatcher. $8°$ pp. 28.
Boston: Re-printed by Thomas Fleet, jun. MDCCXCVI.

For first edition, 1728, see page 48.

Essays to do Good, Addressed to all Christians. By the late Cotton Mather. A New Edition improved by George Burder. $8°$ pp. 195 (1).
Johnstown: Printed and Sold by Asa Child. 1815.

For the edition of 1808 and one without date, see page 49.

Early Piety: Exemplified in the Life and Death of Mr. Nathaniel Mather. $12°$ pp. 74.
Boston. [1857.]

INCREASE MATHER.

The Life and Death of that Reverend Man of God, Mr. Richard Mather, Teacher of the Church in Dorchester in New England. $4°$ pp. (4), 38.
Cambridge: Printed by S. G. and M. J. 1670.

The Times of Men are in the hand of God. Or a Sermon occasioned by that awfull Providence which hapned [sic] in Boston in New England, the 4th day of the 3d Moneth, 1675, (when part of a vessel was blown up in the Harbour, and nine men hurt, and three mortally wounded) wherein is shewed how we should sanctifie the dreadfull Name of God under such awfull Dispensations. By Increase Mather, Teacher of a Church of Christ. $4°$ pp. (6), 21.
Boston: Printed by John Foster. 1675.

The Judgment of Several Eminent Divines of the Congregational Way Concerning a Pastors Power Occasionally to Exert Ministerial Acts in another Church, besides that which is His Own Particular Flock. $8°$ $pp.$ (2), 18.
Boston Printed by Benjamin Harris, and are to be Sold by Richard Wilkins. 1693.

De Successu Evangelii Apud Indos in Novâ-Angliâ Epistola. Ad Cl. Virum D. Johannem Leusdenum. A Crescentio Mathero. $8°$ $pp.$ (2), 13.
Londini, Typis J. G. 1688.

Some Remarks on a Pretended Answer, to a Discourse concerning the Common-Prayer Worship. With an Exhortation to the Churches in New-England, to hold fast the Profession of their Faith without Wavering. By Increase Mather, D. D. $8°$ $pp.$ 36. *Appendix* (2), 10.
Printed for Nath. Hillier at the Princes Arm's in Leaden-Hall-Street, in London: and for the Book-sellers in Boston, in New-England. [1712].

Burnings Bewailed: in a Sermon, Occasioned by the Lamentable Fire which was in Boston, Octob. 2, 1711. In which the Sins which Provoke the Lord to Kindle Fires, are Enquired into. By Increase Mather, D.D. $8°$ $pp.$ (4), 36.
Boston Printed: Sold by Timothy Green. 1711.
For second edition, 1712, see page 29.

MOSES MATHER.

The Visible Church, in Covenant with God; Further Illustrated. Containing Also, A brief Representation of some other Gospel-Doctrines, which affect the Controversy. By Moses Mather, A. M. $8°$ $pp.$ 84.
New Haven: Printed by Thomas and Samuel Green, in the Old-Council Chamber. MDCCLXX.

NATHANAEL MATHER.

1686. The Boston Ephemeris. An Almanack of Cœlestial Motions of the Sun & Planets, with some of the principal Aspects. For the Year of the Christian Æra MDCLXXXVI. Being in our Account the third after Leap-year, and from the Creation 5635. By Nathanael Mather. $12°$ $pp.$ 16.
New-England, Boston, Printed and Sold by Samuel Green, 1686.

SAMUEL MATHER (OF BOSTON).

A Modest Account concerning the Salutations and Kissings in ancient Times: Wherein Mr. Sandeman's Attempt, to revive the holy and charitable Kiss, and the Love-Feasts, is considered: By Constant Rock-man, M. A. $8°$ $pp.$ 19.
Boston: N. E. MDCCLXVIII.

The Sacred Minister: a new Poem, in five Parts; Representing his Qualifications for the Ministry, And his Life and Death in it. By Aurelius Prudentius, Americanus. $8°$ $pp.$ 23.
Boston, MDCCLXXIII.

Christian Biography. Life of Dr. Cotton Mather. Of Boston, North America. Abridged from the account published by his son, the Rev. Samuel Mather. $12°$ $pp.$ 72. [London] n. d.
See page 50 for edition of 1729.